AGENTS ON ACTORS

AGENTS ON ACTORS

OVER SIXTY PROFESSIONALS
SHARE THEIR SECRETS
ON FINDING WORK
ON THE STAGE AND SCREEN

Hettie Lynne Hurtes

BACK STAGE BOOKS
an imprint of Watson-Guptill Publications/New York

Project Manager: Alisa Palazzo
Copy Editor: Amy Handy
Designer: Cheryl Viker
Production Manager: Hector Campbell

First published in 2000 in New York by Back Stage Books, an imprint of Watson-Guptill
Publications, a division of BPI Communications, Inc., 1515 Broadway, New York, NY 10036

Library of Congress Catalog Card Number: 00-101811

ISBN: 0-8230-8803-0

This book is set in Adobe Garamond, 11pt.

1 2 3 4 5 6 / 05 04 03 02 01 00

Manufactured in the United States of America

This book is dedicated to my family—
Ron and our three children, Jennifer, Aubrey, and Brandon.

They allowed me the uninterrupted time each day to
devote to my writing, kept me on schedule, and prevented me from
indulging in procrastination. (If I didn't get my work done,
I couldn't go out and play.) Thanks guys. You're the best!

Contents

Additional Resources

Introduction

What image does the word *agent* conjure up for you? Is it a portly cigar-munching man in his fifties, sitting behind a big desk, or perhaps an intimidating woman with a phone in one hand and an attitude in the other? After interviewing more than sixty agents from Los Angeles to New York, I can tell you that agents come in a variety of sizes, shapes, and colors, and they're no different from any other group of businesspeople. Some are warm, and some are on the cool side of the spectrum. There are theatrical agents who are young, and there are those who've been around for decades. The one thing they all have in common is the need for actors. Actors are their raison d'être, their sine qua non, if you will, and while some will be forthright and let you know they're working for you, others may lead you to believe the opposite. I've heard actors bemoan the fact that they have to do all the work, while their agents rake in their 10 percent.

How many actors do you know who praise their agents? How many times have you heard actors tell you how great their agents are, constantly submitting photos and sending them out on a slew of auditions? The truth is, you don't hear that as frequently as you hear the gripes and groans of actors threatening to find a new agent to make their dreams come true. Well, actors, here's the nitty-gritty: Agents can only do so much for the actor. Their role in this often frustrating industry is to submit a client's photo and resume and negotiate a contract should the actor get the job. Of course most agents worth their salt put a lot more effort into the process, but basically, that's their function. Hoping for more? You may want to hire a manager, but that's another book. . . .

Agents on Actors attempts to clarify a lot of the mystique surrounding "agenting." As you read each profile on a specific agent, you'll learn more about not only what the agent does but what you, the actor, can do to accelerate the process of becoming a "working actor." The one thing you should keep in mind as you're reading the book is that every agent I've included is a franchised agent. That means the agent is registered with one or more of the major guilds: SAG (Screen Actors Guild), AFTRA (American Federation of Television and Radio Artists), and AEA (Actors Equity Association). This is very important when selecting an agent. If your agent is not franchised with the guilds, you're not likely to go out on any union auditions. In most cities, union members are required to deal only with franchised agents and vice versa. There are hundreds of franchised agents across the country, and as you can imagine, mainstream casting directors, dealing with network television and feature films, are not going to call an agent who isn't acknowledged by the unions. Why should they? They're pros and they want to deal with other pros. Anyone can become a manager, but if you want to call yourself a professional talent agent, you have to be under the aegis of the guilds.

You may wonder if you have to be in the union to obtain a franchised agent. The answer is no, with reservations. It's difficult to get a good agent even if you're in the union, so if you're new and haven't had much experience, it's even tougher. Fortunately there's something called the Taft-Hartley Act, which allows an actor the chance to appear in a union production as long as he or she joins the union prior to working on a subsequent job. Therefore, if an agent sees potential, he or she may sign the young actor, hoping that it won't take long to get that Taft-Hartley rule working for the new client.

In order for agents to become franchised, applicants must demonstrate that theirs is a legitimate business registered with the state or city, and that they maintain a proper office space, surety bonds, and client trust accounts. Agents are also supposed to demonstrate thorough knowledge of the entertainment business. It's not an easy process. Once an agent becomes franchised, he or she may not charge a higher rate of commission than 10 percent of the actor's gross earnings and may only get that commission when and if the actor is compensated for the job. Agents may not—and this is very important to understand—charge up-front fees of any kind or require you to go to a specific acting school or use a specific photographer as a condition of representation.

So, what can you expect from your agent? A good agent will only handle the number of actors of which he or she can properly keep track. That doesn't mean the William Morris Agency or ICM, which handle hundreds of clients, can't possibly do a good job. On the contrary, larger agencies often employ many agents and subagents who help handle the workload. If the agents are doing their job, they'll either split the clients between them or divide up the studios and other contacts so that each agent isn't biting off more than he or she can chew. Smaller agencies or boutiques, as they're sometimes called, may have one or two agents who handle a select number of clients, sometimes only fifty or so, but they may not have the luxury of splitting up their tasks. In other words, having a small or large agency behind you isn't what's important. What is important is that you have a good relationship with your particular agent.

According to nearly all the agents with whom I've talked, communication is vital. If you're not happy with your agent, for whatever reason, you shouldn't be afraid to go in and get it off your chest. If you're afraid, because every time you call you can't even get through to your agent, who never returns your call, perhaps it's time to think about looking elsewhere for representation. But if you're disgruntled and your agent is willing to have you come in and chat, you shouldn't put it off. You, the actor, are expected to do some of the legwork, but if you're doing that and still haven't heard from your agent in a month or two, it's time to find out why.

Many of the agents interviewed in this book complain that actors turn in their resignations without so much as a single attempt to discuss their situation. If they've put time and effort into furthering your career, they feel the least an actor can do is give them some feedback.

There are agents who function simply as submitters and contract writers, while others prefer to maintain a close relationship with each person they represent, in a somewhat managerial capacity. Most agents seem to fall between the two extremes. They will not only submit an actor if Breakdown Services* posts a casting notice for someone of his or her type, but will often get on the phone and call a director, producer, or casting person, enthusiastically suggesting the actor for a specific part. And this is where one agency will dominate another in the popularity poll among actors. Who wouldn't rather have an agent with enough clout to get clients in on a major audition rather than one who never gets a phone call returned? But, alas, life being what it is, it may take time to attract a hotshot agent. Until then, there's a lot you, the actor, can do to supplement your agent's efforts. This book will guide you through the steps.

Be aware that there are two ways you can be represented: by signing a contract with an agent or by freelancing. On the East Coast it's more common for an actor to have a variety of agents and let the chips fall as they may, whereas on the West Coast most agents require a contract. Just because you're signed with an agent doesn't necessarily mean you can't get out of the contract. You may obtain a release under certain circumstances, which your agent or union can explain to you, but all terminations must be in writing. You can always check with the unions if there's a dispute.

A good website for actors considering an agent is www.aftra.com/resources/ agents. Here you'll get a succinct introduction, explaining what agents are, how to find one, how to submit to an agent, and the difference between agents and managers. Check it out if you have access to the World Wide Web. Enjoy *Agents on Actors,* and good luck with your acting career!

*BREAKDOWN SERVICES is a fee-based service provided to agents that offers a daily breakdown of roles for each production submitted by participating casting directors.

THE AGENTS

Michael Amato

1650 Broadway, #307
New York, NY 10019
(212) 247-4456
FAX (212) 664-0641

Have you ever heard of the Duprees? Probably not, unless you were around in the '50s. The Duprees were a popular singing group, and Michael Amato was one of the teenage trillers who got his start on the street corners of New Jersey. When the group's popularity began to wane, Amato decided he'd like to be a manager of other young talent looking to be discovered. He found that helping others to succeed suited him, so eventually he decided to expand his horizons and become an agent. "There are very few good agents," he professes. "For that reason, actors have to do a lot of work on their own. There are agents who don't even know how to negotiate a deal. They're afraid." Amato seems unafraid of almost anything. He has been doing this since 1979, and nothing seems to intimidate him. When "they" told him he had to change his name when he first started in the business, he laughed. "I'm Italian. Why should I change my name?"

Amato represents sports celebrities as well as actors, including Yogi Berra, Walt Frazier, Phil Rizzuto, and Bill Boggs. He is also known for his fine list of ethnic actors, another thing "they" told him would hurt his career. Now ethnic actors are his bread and butter. One of his clients is Asian actor Billy Chang, of *New York Undercover* and *Law and Order,* who has been with him nine years. "Without a contract," he notes. "I don't believe in contracts between actors and agents. If the person's not happy, I don't want him or her. It's that simple." He realizes that actors are going to move on when they're ready, whether or not there's a contract. He cites former clients Ramon Franco of *Tour of Duty* and Steven James of *Delta Force.* "A small agency is only a stepping stone," he admits. "When they've built up enough credits, they move on. That's the business."

Fortunately for Amato, he doesn't have to seek out clients. They come to him. "And I don't take on an actor because of a resume. I want to see a demo tape." If actors don't have tape, Amato may take them on in the print department or send them out on nonunion projects. Most theatrical agents don't handle print, but Amato enjoys it. He says it's very profitable, as well as satisfying, when he can help a new actor find work. He has even gotten work for his brother-in-law and his eighty-five-year-old mother before she passed away. "They get their feet wet in print and start feeling comfortable in front of the camera."

Amato also recommends that beginners do showcases and join theater groups in order to hone their craft, but not necessarily to attract an industry audience. In fact, Amato rarely goes to showcases himself. "I'd rather spend my free time helping homeless animals." As for formal training, he's not an advocate of acting schools. "I think their popularity is overrated. They overcharge actors. It's ridiculous! Show business is the biggest scam in the world," he warns. "I'm from the old school. You and other actor friends form a theater group and develop your skills." Once in a while he'll find a good teacher like Jim Moody (of *Bad Boys*), who teaches at La Guardia High School and gives private lessons in his spare time for a minimal amount of money. "Jim will tell me when an actor is prepared to be sent out on auditions. If he gives me the okay, I know the actor's ready to go."

In addition, Amato shies away from brownnosing. "I refuse to wine and dine casting directors to get my clients in the door. I find it doesn't work. If you have the talent they need, they're going to call you whether they like you or not, because they have to produce. I used to send gifts to people after they hired my talent, and you know what? I never heard from them again. I used to take casting directors to lunch at Sardi's in a chauffeured limousine. It never worked. I don't think they like it. It's not professional."

Having actors who fit the bill is his real goal. Amato is proud to have been the first to recognize the talent of several actors who've gone on to big careers. He recalls meeting Esai Morales (of *La Bamba* fame) when the actor was sixteen, and Marlon Wayans, who he predicted could be another Richard Pryor if he worked hard. Working hard includes not only continuing to become good at what you do, but also marketing yourself. "One of my actors buys the *Hollywood Reporter* and *Variety* every day and sends out his photos to all the production houses that have movies coming out. He gets calls all the time. He doesn't depend on me for everything. It has to be teamwork."

The most frustrating part of Amato's job, he says, is working with certain people who "appear to know it all" but don't. "One actor I offered to represent without signing didn't like the offer. He left and came back a year later. He had signed with another agent and nothing happened. I told him I knew he'd be back. He asked me to work with him, but once an actor balks at an offer I've made, it's over." He's also frustrated that agents aren't more respected by the industry as a whole. If he had one wish, it would be for agents to share the limelight at the Academy Awards. "Why shouldn't we get Oscars too?"

Karen Apicella

FRONTIER BOOKING
1560 Broadway, #1110
New York, NY 10036
(212) 221-0220
FAX (212) 221-0821

Karen Apicella has always wanted to be "in the business." When she attended Columbia University, she was immediately attracted to the campus radio station. Not only did she have her own show, she was also designated publicity director for the station. After graduation she tried her hand—make that her vocal chords—at professional radio, but she found that merely being a voice wasn't as rewarding as doing it all. "I much preferred the producing side, so I decided to get a job with an ad agency. At the time, they didn't have a production job available, and I ended up working for the casting directors." She loved it. From that time on, she knew she wanted to work with actors.

Frontier Booking is a music and talent agency in New York. The high-profile music division represents artists like Sting, Snoop Dog, and Jane's Addiction. The talent division is relatively small with only three agents, but Apicella is comfortable there, primarily representing youngsters and young adults from birth to age thirty. "When you start looking like you could have your own kids, you're too old for us," she quips. Frontier prefers people in their twenties who can look like teens. That's always a winning combination, even for the younger set. "Looking younger is a very big plus right now," she stresses.

Frontier has both a commercial and a theatrical department, with an emphasis on commercial, since New York has limited television or movie opportunities on a regular basis. The agency does some legitimate theater, but that, too, isn't where its strength lies. "One of our clients was in the original cast of [the recent Broadway production of] *The Sound of Music*," she recalls, "and she's still with us. But it's not often that there are roles for young people on Broadway." Some clients are strong singers but weak actors and vice versa, although, Apicella admits, "It's always easier to sell someone who can do it all." Singers aren't hired just for the theater. Even though jingles are primarily handled by music production houses, the agency does get calls for kids. "Kids who sing aren't very common. Those who can take direction get work a lot." Of course, that holds true across the board, for every age group and in every aspect of the business.

Apicella says if you're a guy, you're more likely to get work. "It's indicative of the world," she comments. "Even for kids, for the most part. *Buffy the Vampire Slayer* is an exception. The ratio is equal on that show, but in commercials and elsewhere there are just more calls for men and boys." Some of her male clients, however, don't stay in the business; after a few years they decide that playing sports is more fun. "One of my clients loved to audition. Then when he got a little older, he got into team sports. He had to miss practices because of auditions, so he asked his mom if he could drop out. Being a good parent, she said fine." That's one of the hazards of working with kids. "Kids go in and out of this business, whereas most adults make it a career choice from the outset." Apicella recalls a female client who was in high gear with her commercial career. "She was about to complete her junior year in high school when her grades started slipping, and she was always missing her math classes, too. The proverbial straw that broke the camel's back was when she and her mom, who'd never done any acting, were asked to audition for a mother-daughter commercial. The mom got it and she didn't. They took it as a sign, and she's not actively pursuing the business any longer."

According to Apicella, kids seem to actually take the rejection better than their parents. "The youngsters don't usually care if they get the job or not. They're doing it for fun and they go with the flow. The parents, on the other hand, take it much harder." She believes it's up to the parents to teach the child what's really important in life. "We try to remind parents that this is their kid's childhood, not their career." About half her clients drop out by the time they're adults; the other half is happy to continue. "We do have those kids who are driven and can't imagine doing anything else with their lives. The ones who have the temperament to do this sort of thing are the ones who go in, do the audition, do their best, and then put it out of their minds. If they get a callback, it's a happy surprise. If they don't, they've already forgotten about it, and they don't dwell on it."

As far as studying is concerned, Apicella feels that it depends on the age of the actor. "A seven-year-old should be natural and doesn't need classes. When you're seventeen, you need to know what to do with your talent. You can't just charm people anymore. You have to be able to act." Little ones, she feels, are natural actors. "Classes often make you think too much about what you're doing, and once that happens, you aren't acting." For teens, however, she believes classes can help, not only to teach you how to channel your talent but to figure out if you want to put in the hours of hard work this career requires.

Working with young people isn't always easy. "There's always a major crisis going on," she admits, and it's up to her to fix it. "It's always exciting and always different, but it's not always fun." The best piece of advice Apicella can give actors is this: "To be successful in this industry is to love it. If you can picture yourself doing anything else, then do it, because this business provides no guarantees. It's not based on merit. It's simply being in the right place at the right time with the right stuff."

Holly Baril

WILLIAM MORRIS AGENCY
151 El Camino Drive
Beverly Hills, CA 90212
(310) 859-4442
FAX (310) 859-4576

Holly Baril has been in the industry for nine years. Originally from New Orleans, she majored in journalism at the University of Texas. She dreamed of becoming a great writer, but soon realized it wasn't her dream alone but that of everyone else in the romantic environs of New Orleans. So when she was offered a job at Rogers and Cowan, a major public relations firm in Los Angeles, she decided to give it a shot. "I hated it. I was put in charge of a number of B movies, and all I did was go to screenings of horror films, sitting through six screenings of the same movie. It was exhausting!" Next? "I thought being an agent might require more creativity, working from the ground up, reading scripts, looking for material for clients, and developing careers." After doing some research, she aptly chose William Morris Agency, because at that time many of the powerful female agents had just left to go elsewhere, and she saw that as a window of opportunity.

It didn't take Baril long before she was the assistant to the head of the television department, which she favored over film because of its business orientation. "It's about numbers, and I liked that." But when she was promoted to episodic television, where she handled some lower-level and "favor" clients who were friends of agents or relatives of powerful clients, she knew she had to take control and develop her own protégés. "It was a wonderful evolution," she says. "I was finally able to sign some terrific actors such as Jordana Brewster, Eddie Cibrian, and Tiffani-Amber Thiessen. When Eddie came to me, he had a little-known film on his reel called *Living Out Loud.* I first saw him in the daytime magazines. He was a regular on *Sunset Beach.* I knew if he could act, he'd be a major star." It wasn't easy for Baril to sign a new actor, since young agents didn't usually have that privilege, but the agency trusted her intuition. "I shopped him around the networks, which all offered development deals, and after one movie audition, we signed a three-picture deal."

Enticing former *Beverly Hills 90210* star Tiffani-Amber Thiessen to William Morris was another coup for Baril, but the ambitious agent wanted to see this talented actress expand her horizons. "What I like to do," she admits, "is take actors I believe are incredible and put them on a career path. If they're known for TV, I'll help them get into film. I also want to keep my talent financially stable so that they don't have to do a project they don't want to do just because they need the money. They should be comfortable so that they can make educated choices or go to New York and do theater for six months if they want to." She's proud that none of her clients have day jobs.

For Baril, it's not as much about the money as it is about the security. "There are three reasons to do a job: the career, the soul, and the money. If you can't find a really good reason to do something, don't!" She has about forty major clients, on whom she focuses most of her attention, and while many agents shy away from personal relationships with actors, Baril takes a different approach. "I'm close with most of my clients. I socialize with them, even travel with them. I [helped] Peri Gilpin [Roz from *Frasier*] pick out gowns for her family for her wedding." If an actor's manager suggests that the actor distance himself or herself from Baril, she'll opt to drop the client. "Why get involved in a power struggle?" she asks. "It's easier to back out of the relationship."

Actors today need not choose a single medium in which to work. Baril believes actors should do lots of good theater. "I grew up watching bus and truck tours coming through New Orleans, and I think actors are missing a good opportunity to grow and learn new techniques if they just stick to film and TV." Crossovers are now common in all areas; actors like George Clooney and Helen Hunt are doing television and film simultaneously. In Baril's view, what's important is getting as much experience in as many areas as possible while you're young. Training, too, is vital. "It's especially important for lesser-known actors. You have to stay in class, get coached, don't stop learning. If you don't put in the work, it's going to show."

Baril's pet peeves include dishonesty. "Lying on resumes about references and about age is bad news for an actor interested in representation," she insists. "I understand and appreciate ambition, but lying is unacceptable." Overinflated egos are a path to rejection by Baril and her colleagues. "I know we all have egos in this business, but I don't want to represent people who are unrealistic about themselves. Ambition is good, but don't make me laugh at you." She's so careful about whom she'll sign, she makes sure to check with studios, directors, and sometimes previous agents to get a better idea of the person she's considering. "I've been burned. Actors may look great on tape and handle an interview well, but I've seen some turn around and be so aggressive on the set that they're fired from every job they book." It's vital for actors to remember their manners and behavior. "You're there to act, not to preen and flex your muscles, unless they're your acting muscles. Never yell at a production assistant either, because you never know what that PA may become in the future."

Baril takes her time signing clients, and when she does make that commitment, she's loyal to the end. "You can have a team of people working for you," she offers, "but if they aren't passionate about you, guess what? Nothing happens. That's why you have to sign people for the right reasons. It's about passion." For the actor, it's about hard work, and she has no time for those who don't take this business seriously. "Work begets work. You have to find the rhythm of being in this business. Luck aside, work speaks for itself."

Marian Berzon

336 East 17th Street
Costa Mesa, CA 92627
(949) 631-5936
FAX (949) 631-6881

Is it possible to be a successful Los Angeles agent and not live in Los Angeles? Just ask Marian Berzon, who had been told for years that having an office in Orange County, fifty miles to the south, was just plain ridiculous. "I'll never forget the time a client and I went up to Los Angeles to meet the director of *Barney Miller,* whom he knew from New York and hoped would give him an opportunity to read for the show. I handed him my business card, which he immediately handed back, saying, 'I don't call area code 714.'" But instead of disillusioning Berzon, these negative comments only provided fuel for her fire. "I said, The more you tell me I'll be out of business, the harder I'm going to work to prove you all wrong."

Being located behind the proverbial "Orange Curtain" has provided its share of frustrations and challenges, but Berzon has persevered and is now recognized as a viable contender. So why did she choose to be so far from the "action"? When she first immigrated to Southern California from New York, she and her husband settled in a suburb of Los Angeles. Unfortunately her husband was transferred to Kansas City, and when that job came to an end a month later, they decided to settle in Newport Beach. Berzon was an actress at the time and was encouraged to study commercial technique and try to break into that field. "The workshop where I was studying wasn't organized at all, and I offered to help. I worked there for four years and built up a pretty good reputation as a casting director in the area." The one drawback for her was that these jobs were local. She also didn't approve of the practice of having an actor sign up for expensive acting classes with the promise of getting work. She finally quit and opened her own talent agency. Many of her clients came with her, and once she obtained her union franchise, she was ready to go.

One of Berzon's logistical concerns was being able to afford to ship her clients' photos and resumes up to Los Angeles casting directors on time every day. An entrepreneurial client had an idea, which turned out to be the perfect answer. He stored all the pictures in his Los Angeles apartment. After going through the daily breakdowns, Berzon would fax him her choices and he would gather them, and a messenger would pick them up and deliver them. She's still doing business that way, and it apparently works well. "I'm in at 7:30 every morning," she says. "I have nearly eight hundred clients, so I need to be very organized. I have all my clients' pictures out on shelves, separated into industrial, theatrical, children." Together,

Berzon and her assistant handle all the areas she represents, including live trade shows, print, and voice-overs. But she doesn't complain. She's used to the frenetic pace, and when one area is less busy, another segment is bound to need attention. "It's never slow," she boasts. "My clients are thrilled, because they have the opportunity to work in L.A. and Orange County. If it's slow for them in television, they can always come down here and do an industrial or print."

Berzon deals directly with advertising agencies in Orange County. She has a great rapport with the producers, since she handles so many high-caliber actors, and they respect her. "My attitude is different from a lot of agents up north. I like to have fun while I work. I believe in communicating. If a client calls me every day, I'm going to talk to that person. It's so tough out there, if an actor is alone and can't interact with the agent, it's pretty sad." Not only will she accept calls from her clients, she is often more excited than they are when they book a job. "I have an eighty-year-old actress, Marge Anderson, who was up for a feature film in which she was supposed to play a sickly old lady in a nursing home. Marge isn't sickly at all, but I knew she could do it. She booked it; her first job since she'd been out here from Chicago, where she'd worked all the time. I thanked the casting people a million times for giving this woman an opportunity."

Many agents won't take on actors who seem similar, for fear of having them compete against each other, but Berzon disagrees with this strategy. "I don't believe in conflicts. No two people are completely alike. I don't care how similar you are, you approach things differently. I don't categorize. When I look at a breakdown, I read into the character, look at my pictures, and select who I want to submit. It's that simple." If an actor isn't booking, Berzon may suggest a good acting coach. In Los Angeles she recommends Sal Romeo, Greg Franklin, and others on her list. The two she respects in Orange County are Ron Michaelson and Elizabeth Kent. "I think actors should attend one class and meet the teacher to see if he or she is suitable for them. I can't make that decision. It's personal." The same holds true for headshot photographers. She offers a list, but it's up to the actor to make the ultimate decision.

If there's one disagreeable aspect to this business for Berzon, it's disloyalty. "I took on an actor from New York. He was a great character type, and I worked my tail off for him. He booked a lot of television with recurring roles. One day he asked if I could help him find a manager. Not only did I find him a good manager, but the two of us managed to get him a series. Then after thirteen weeks he called and said, 'Well, I'm moving on.' I said, 'Pardon me?' I felt betrayed. But his disloyalty was aptly rewarded. The following week, he was cancelled from the show." As they say, what goes around, comes around.

David Brady

THE TALENT GROUP
Partners: Pat Brannon
and Judy Rich
6300 Wilshire Boulevard, #2110
Los Angeles, CA 90048
(213) 852-9559
FAX (213) 852-9579

David Brady's story is definitely one of Hollywood proportions. His dad, a television producer and network executive, told him that the only person he knew who made a living in the business—receiving a weekly paycheck—was his agent. So, Dad set up an appointment for his son with the International Famous Agency, and not surprisingly, Brady was on the first rung of his ladder. "In fact," Brady recalls, "I was the guy who delivered the agreement that merged our agency with CMA, which became ICM [International Creative Management]," and with the merger, Brady was granted the job of handling their insurance. "I kind of became the pope of ICM, because I knew everybody's personal life. I was doing their insurance, so I was gaining their confidence."

Before long, Brady was heading up the commercials department at the agency. "It was ridiculous. I was twenty-one and had no idea what I was doing." On his suggestion, they brought in an expert, who very quickly overshadowed Brady. Needless to say, Brady left for more autonomous pastures. He wasn't at his new job more than three months when a major agency invited him to head up their commercials department. Feeling that he would be betraying his new partner, he turned down the offer, only to learn the meaning of back stabbing when this partner informed him a few weeks later that he was leaving for that very same plum position! "That was my first experience of being royally screwed," Brady confesses. Not one to collapse in the face of adversity, Brady picked up the phone and was soon offered a job at Abrams Rubaloff, another major commercial agency in Los Angeles. He was there four and a half years until Joan Mangum, a successful print agent, invited him to become a partner and develop the commercial end of her business. "That was in 1981. Today it's me, Pat Brannon, and Judy Rich. Joan is still on board as a consultant."

Brady handles celebrity clients while Brannon and Rich are responsible for on-camera and administrative duties. Under the aegis of Wes Stevens, they also have a top-notch voice-over department, which has helped establish The Talent Group as one of the foremost talent agencies on the West Coast. "The person who really put us on the map," says Brady, "was John Corbett of *Northern Exposure.*

We made a deal for him as the voice of Isuzu. Once that happened, other celebrities started coming on board." Brady believes the celebrity bandwagon started when film directors such as Ridley Scott and Adrian Lyne wanted to get into the commercial field. "I think that gave a quality to commercials that had never been there before." Now everyone seems to want to get into the act, he says. "It's a feeding frenzy with directors like David Lynch, the Coen Brothers, and John Frankenheimer shooting commercials."

Nowadays, in addition to voice-over commercials, celebrities want to do major animated features, and The Talent Group handles many of those celebrity voices. "Animation has become a huge business for us, because theatrical agencies don't want to pursue it. They're working on film deals and television deals; the last thing they need is to have to bring in actors and record their voices in a sound booth. We do it twenty-four hours a day." And yes, celebrities have to audition, too. "Rarely is an offer made without the producer or agency hearing the voice on tape. If they're going to spend huge amounts of money, they want to know the actor's able to do the job." Brady says that most actors are happy to come in and read. "We're blessed, because our clients think it's fun. They don't consider it insulting. We wouldn't want actors with egos so big they can't realize that reading is part of the process."

There are even instances when stars lose out to scale talent. "We booked a guy on a Sherwin-Williams campaign that included radio and TV spots," Brady recalls. "It was cast in New York, L.A., and Chicago. Every celebrity came in and read for it, but it went to scale talent. Many times I've been in serious discussions about a celebrity they didn't end up hiring; they wound up selecting a scale performer instead." Not only do the producers save hundreds of thousands of dollars, they may even discover a new talent. "John Corbett actually started out doing commercials. That's how he got noticed for *Northern Exposure*," Brady explains. "He was so spectacular in commercials everyone wanted to know who he was. I think one of the spots was a jack-in-the-box where he did this natural kind of read up close. It started his career."

Brady doesn't believe there's such thing as the "commercial actor" today. "We don't want someone who doesn't have a theatrical range. Those generic commercials we used to see, the pitches, are in the minority today. The majority of big campaigns use people who are like those you'd see on *NYPD Blue* or *ER*. We have actors who go in and out of series and commercials. They don't give up commercials today just because they have a series running. They just can't see throwing it away anymore. They like the income." A good example of the atypical commercial spokesperson is Jonathan Pryce, the Broadway actor. "When Jonathan got the Infinity campaign, they were looking all over the world for someone unusual, without a TVQ. They didn't care that he was a two-time Tony Award winner who won Best Actor in Cannes for *Carrington*. They just wanted a class act. But that campaign has definitely helped Jonathan gain recognition in the American film scene."

The Talent Group really believes in marketing its clients. "We let advertising agencies know where and when our clients are performing. When someone is visiting Europe, we'll set up meetings for the person over there." The agency even has two websites to promote its talent. "The one that is most innovative is the voice-over website," boasts Brady. "That enables us to provide the specs of what a producer is looking for. Say they're seeking someone fifty with a Cajun accent and good sense of humor. Via e-mail, the site will spit out a list of people who'd fall into that category." Users can also download voice samples onto the website, so producers can hear the actor without having to request a tape. "And then there's the ISDN line that enables us to send studio-quality recordings to ad agencies from anywhere in the world. It's amazing!"

The case of Jonathan Pryce clinching the Infinity account is an example of how technology can benefit the actor, agency, and producer. Pryce was in Spain shooting a film when the ad agency decided they wanted to do a screen test. Chiat Day flew in an account executive from Europe who brought a camera crew from a local news station to the remote Spanish village. "Jonathan was on a night shoot and hadn't gotten much sleep. He walked onto the balcony and shot the test. They flew the tape back to Madrid that night and sent it by satellite to Chiat Day's boardroom in L.A. for the client to see. The agency viewed the tape and hired Pryce, all in a matter of hours."

The Talent Group isn't currently seeking clients. Its clients are mostly from referrals, but that's not to say they don't look at pictures and resumes that come in to the office. "We can never not open an envelope," Brady admits, "because you never know what's inside." It's part of the job, part of what makes The Talent Group one of the major players in town. They refuse to overlook any possibility, and they're proud of their success and reputation. "I think our office success is based on our modesty. We're not flashy. We don't brag about what we do. But one thing we've decided is that we always have to move forward. We can't stop. If we remain stagnant, if we don't contemporize our office technology, we'll start losing. So we have to stay one step ahead of the game at all times."

Maureen Brookman

STEWART TALENT
58 West Huron Street
Chicago, IL 60610
(312) 943-3226
FAX (312) 943-5107

Maureen Brookman has been an agent in Chicago for eighteen years. Prior to that she worked in New York as merchandise editor for *Glamour* magazine. As is so often the case in the entertainment industry, she and Jane Stewart met at a cocktail party. "Jane wanted to start a children's print division at her agency, and since I had three children myself, she figured I was a good choice." Brookman is the director of this full-service agency, which specializes in on-camera commercial, theatrical, voice-over, and commercial print. They handle about sixty-five actors on an exclusive basis and about two hundred or so on a freelance basis. Of those, a third are also handled by affiliate agencies in New York or Los Angeles. The main focus of the agency, she says, is to develop talent. "We've helped several major actors get started, including Chris O'Donnell and Robin Tunney. I figured out early that I wasn't merely going to hand them off to New York or Los Angeles. So we have business agreements with agencies in those cities. They place the actors, and we get a percentage of the commission." They only do this with those they handle exclusively.

Chris O'Donnell was only ten years old when he walked in to Stewart Talent. "I looked at his father and said, "He's going to make forty thousand dollars this year, because he's a perfect size twelve." The celebrity news shows often call Brookman for old photos of him in pajamas, which she vows she'll never release. "I remember his first film job when he was sixteen, *Men Don't Leave*. He missed the audition three times. I called his mother and told her to bribe him, to do whatever she could to get him there. That was the beginning."

The agency is always scouting for new talent. "I send my associates to colleges like Northwestern and DePaul to see their showcases. We also get referrals from casting directors and other agents, and we get lots of submissions in the mail. One of our associates does nothing but scout actors and put them on tape for me." The selection process is rigid. "You can't just drop off a picture and resume at our door and expect to be seen." If your headshot does come through the mail, however, and they like it, you may get a call to come in and audition, at which point you'll be asked to do a monologue or read some commercial copy. It's important for Brookman to know that an actor can do a good cold reading. The agency even has a booth to put together voice-over auditions for clients.

Many national commercials shoot in Chicago, which also has its share of television and feature films. "Joan Cusack is hopefully bringing a half-hour sitcom here. *Early Edition* starring Kyle Chandler has been picked up for twenty-two episodes. Joan's brother, John, and Bonnie Hunt are both doing movies here. There's also a fair amount of independent filmmaking going on. It's probably the best place for an actor to get started. That's why we encourage kids just out of school not to go running off to Los Angeles or New York, but to spend at least a year here and see what happens." She also encourages actors to take advantage of the area's wealth of theater training, such as the Goodman, the Steppenwolf, and Second City.

Brookman maintains good relationships with casting directors in New York and Los Angeles. She submits directly to casting directors when she feels her actors are right for a particular project. Last year she had a talent reel compiled to submit to casting directors in other cities. "We showed monologues and snippets of work from about a dozen of our top people." She tries to stay competitive and hopes things pick up this year. "Last year it was all teens. I had a twenty-year-old no one wanted to see, because she was too old! I try to submit against type. The voice-over department will send out a female comedian for a male voice-over, and nine times out of ten, she'll beat out the males."

The agency prides itself on having a loyal clientele. "People who come to us don't leave," she boasts. "We take care of them. Our style is very nurturing. I went to Chris O'Donnell's wedding. We're like family. We have the luxury to be able to do that. Our commercials and industrials pay the bills, so we have time to develop our talent for film and television." She admits that it may not be the most practical way to go, from a business standpoint, but she says she's in it for the long haul. "We don't just throw them against the wall and see what sticks. We want to help them have the careers that they've always dreamed of and deserve."

W. Randolph Clark

13415 Ventura Boulevard, #3
Sherman Oaks, CA 91423
(818) 385-0583
FAX (818) 385-0599

Step into Randy Clark's office, and you're stepping back in time into one of the most unusual agent offices in Los Angeles, with retro furniture and autographed photos of stars like Ann Miller. Clark is known for possessing a rather unique clientele. "I found out early on," he explains, "that if you specialize in a certain type of actor, the casting directors will know to call you for those particular types." And specialize he does. Not only has he a file of talented children, he also has an extensive senior division. "When I started in the '80s, I discovered that actors in their twenties, thirties, and forties could be somewhat disloyal once they became successful, so I decided to focus on children and young adults. They were more apt not to cancel an audition because of a day job, and they appreciated my efforts." The senior division came about when Clark realized there was a need for someone to focus on roles for older actors in film, television, and commercials.

Clark started in theater in the late '60s in Texas. He came out to San Diego to stage manage a touring company of *Lenny* and never went back. He became an agent by accident in the late '70s, when a friend told him of an agency that needed an office assistant. He liked the work, and in 1980 he opened his own agency. "At first we only represented scenic designers, costume designers, and the like. I was a pioneer in that area. At first when I'd make a call, producers would sometimes just hang up. Now producers want all talent to be represented. They don't want to deal directly with 'artistes.'" Although he continues representing below-the-line talent, it wasn't until 1986 that the agency started to represent actors under eighteen and above fifty-five. "We found that many of the older actors had performed when they were younger and were now wanting to get back in the business after careers in other fields like insurance or teaching. Michael Hagen is an example. He was a teacher after being an actor in the '50s. Now he's doing comedy and has appeared several times on HBO's *Mr. Show*."

Clark says the senior market is very competitive. "Other agencies have started picking up older talent. Writers are writing for mature actors now, and not just small parts, either. It's very strong commercially and theatrically." Clark and his associate, Arlene Tsurutani, are very selective with clients. "I know of agencies like us who represent hundreds of clients. I find that impossible. I'd rather have fewer and have them all working." They have to be careful, however, that the senior actors whom they select are not too fragile physically. Some are in their seventies. "I'm very aware of their age and physical condition. They have to be reliable and must have transportation. If they're not in good condition, they won't be able to put in an eight-hour day or longer." He says it's ironic that when you're eighteen they often want you to play younger, but when you're a senior they want you to play older. "A seventy-five-year-old actor who can play eighty-five can make it easier on a production due to his or her physical stamina. It's interesting, but there are many people in top condition at that age," he says. "And there are many more men at that age requesting representation than women."

One of his clients is a celebrity of sorts, especially to Clark. "I've always been fascinated by the space program since I was a child," he admits. "One day I opened a submission that had a photo of an actress named Joan Aldrin. She was the wife of Buzz Aldrin, the second man to go to the moon." She was a working actress with a master's degree in theater, so Clark immediately set up an appointment with her. "She was delightful. When her husband was in the space program, she would run the theater program on the base." Joan Aldrin has been with the agency for several years, and she's apparently doing well in her career. Aside from submissions, Clark finds new clients by word of mouth. Sometimes a client will refer someone, or a casting director may suggest he take a look at an actor looking for representation. He also goes to the theater when one of his clients is appearing in a play, and he'll occasionally find another actor in the cast who's seeking representation.

Clark expects his clients, even seniors, to take a commercial workshop. He also suggests scene study classes and getting involved in a play to keep moving forward in the craft. If an actor hasn't had training, the agency won't be interested. If the actor is a child who hasn't yet taken classes, Clark will recommend a coach. Children fourteen years or older without prior experience in the business are unlikely to find representation with Clark. "It's just difficult to try to compete when there are so many young actors who have already had ten years experience by the time they're teens." There are so many more roles written for kids today, especially in the commercial market, that if Clark had to choose between kids and seniors, he'd have to go with kids because of commercials. "Seniors tend to be stronger theatrically, but the whole balance seems to be ever shifting."

Clark likes the financial rewards of working with young actors but equally enjoys the satisfaction he derives from his older clients. One of his favorite things about working with seniors is their appreciation of the agent's efforts. "It's unusual to hear someone thank you for an audition or even a booking," he admits. "They rarely voice their gratitude; the commission is their thanks. But the seniors always say thank you and report to us on how their audition went. It's very gratifying to have their thanks expressed. It makes my day."

Mary Anne Claro

1513 West Passyunk Avenue
Philadelphia, PA 19145
(215) 465-7788
FAX (215) 465-2747

Throughout her career, Mary Anne Claro has been involved in all aspects of fashion, television, modeling, and radio. Trained by the John Robert Powers Agency in Philadelphia, she was in demand as a runway model because of her ability to communicate to the audience the style and flair of the fashion world. This led the Powers organization to hire Claro as a top instructor and ultimately public relations director. She eventually decided to set up her own agency—one of the longest established modeling and talent agencies in Philadelphia—where she represents talent not just in Pennsylvania, but in New York, Washington, Baltimore, and Virginia as well.

Claro is happy to say that Philadelphia has lots of work for actors commercially and theatrically, but 90 percent of the talent she represents is from New York City. Many of her clients have appeared on such shows as *Loving, As the World Turns,* and *Another World.* Feature films to her credit include *Home Alone Two, Carlito's Way, Rocky I, II, III,* and *Twelve Monkeys.* The agency handles mainly principal casting on big-budget films and is franchised by SAG, AFTRA, and Equity. There are about 140 actors on the roster at any given time. "Every six months," she explains, "I drop about 40 percent of the clientele who are not getting auditions. If I see they're not working, it doesn't pay to keep them on board. They're not making money, and neither am I. It's better for them to move on, perhaps to a smaller agency where they can be better monitored."

Actors interested in hooking up with the Claro Agency can submit a videotape or audio tape as well as their 8x10 and resume. The voice-over department is an integral part of the agency. "I'll set up an appointment with those I'm interested in meeting, and I'll give them an on-camera spot and a voice-over spot to read. If they do well, I'll usually have them come back with a prepared monologue." If an actor who has been in the business a while doesn't have a videotape, Claro will probably turn thumbs down. "If you're just starting out, it's different, since you have nothing to put on tape. But it's an absolute must for anyone who has had experience." She also suggests that a videotape should be no longer than five minutes. "And if you don't get my attention in the first thirty seconds, I'll probably turn it off."

Personality is vital to Claro, whether the actor is an adult or child. "There was this adorable Irish kid who came to see me, eighteen and with lots of personality. The camera could just eat him up. I submitted his name to Mike Lemon

Casting for a job. The intern didn't put him on the list. I called them up and told them they were missing out." They finally agreed to bring him in, along with a six-year-old girl Claro had submitted. They both booked the job.

While most of the casting directors with whom she's associated have no problem working with an out-of-town agent, there are a few for whom she has less than fond feelings. "I remember submitting to a TV show a few years ago, and the casting director called my client directly. When I found out, I was livid and suggested he ask the casting director which photo of the four I submitted was the one they liked. When they showed him the picture, he noticed they had removed the agent's label." She immediately called the casting director to ask why they had done that, but they denied it. "I'll never submit another client to that casting director. It's just a tactic to prevent us from getting our commissions. It happens all the time."

Several casting offices in Philadelphia have a policy of open casting calls, including Mike Lemon, Philadelphia Casting, and Kathy Wickline. Others rely solely on agents submitting for specific projects. Claro always meets with casting companies prior to sending her clients on jobs. "I get in my car and drive to New York to personally meet anyone I will be doing business with. Most people find my approach different, and they respect that. I leave my Fridays open for such meetings." Once she has met the casting director she submits continuously, often for the same project. "I'll submit an actor's picture several times. Sometimes it takes that to get an appointment." Once she gains their respect, they'll usually give her appointments on her first submission.

One of her favorite parts of the job is the voice-over business, which has become one of the most lucrative for the agency. She'll often have her New York talent come to Philadelphia for voice-overs. "One of my clients was getting a thousand dollars per session just to do tags. He booked eight sessions right off the bat." Another client was sent to Scottsdale, Arizona, to do a QVC spokesperson job. "I submitted an actor I knew would be perfect. They didn't call back, but I wouldn't give up. I phoned them and told them I knew they'd be calling a lot of agents, but that my talent was the one who was right for the job. They agreed to see his material, and once they had, they agreed to fly him to Scottsdale to train him, and paid all his expenses plus four hundred dollars per show. They like him so much, they have him working in Tampa, too, and have asked me to supply two backups, since he can't be in both places at the same time."

Claro suggests that her actors keep in touch with casting directors on a frequent basis. "It's a team effort," she insists. "Actors need to send postcards to casting directors every month or so, letting them know what they've been doing," not to mention the need to stay in constant communication with the agency to find out if the agent has enough photos and resumes on hand. "I started out in this business when I was thirteen," she says. "I know an awful lot about it, and I want to share this knowledge with my talent, if they'll listen. I've had much success and happiness, and I hope to continue to have the chance to meet and work with some of the best talent in the industry."

Jacquelyn Conard

SA-RAH TALENT
222 South Morgan Street, #2C
Chicago, IL 60607
(312) 733-2822
FAX (312) 733-1529

Jacquelyn Conard wanted to be a voice-over artist, even though her career initially took her from advertising to production to sales. About a decade ago she suddenly decided to open her own talent agency. If she wasn't going to be the talent, she was going to help others achieve their dreams. "It was really difficult at first," she admits. "Agencies and casting directors don't know you when you're starting out. It takes time to build a reputation. Even in Chicago there's a lot of competition."

Sa-Rah (named after her mother) is a full-service agency handling on-camera and, of course, voice-over work. Since Chicago is a multi-listed town, few of her clients are signed on an exclusive basis. Out of perhaps four thousand actors who seek work through her office, Conard only handles about fifteen, on whom she concentrates her time and effort. "Our commercial actors seem to work the most," she says. "And those who work, work a lot. Our hottest seasons seem to be fall and winter. We're really busy from mid-January to mid-May, then it picks up again right before September and goes through November, just before the holidays."

Sa-Rah prefers a theatrically trained actor with confidence in his or her talent. Because of the wealth of fine theater in Chicago, Conard has a strong roster from which to select. "Unfortunately, while we find actors from the stage, we don't tend to place many in theater. The pay is so small, most theaters hire actors directly. They can't afford to pay an agent commission." Conard attends performances often and will go backstage after the show to introduce herself to those she's interested in representing. "I'll invite them to come to my office to audition and talk about what direction they're looking to go." It's up to both parties whether or not to sign an exclusive contract. "We have to have a rapport, be able to work together, and have some trust and honesty. It's ultimately the actor's decision."

Conard handles a variety of multi-ethnic talent, and according to her, there's ample opportunity for all. Some think that, because she's African-American, she only works with minorities. "I try not to think color when I take on actors. If an actor is qualified and we have a good rapport, we'll work together. If not, we don't. I will try hard to help non-Caucasian actors get a foothold in the business by submitting them to casting directors, hoping they'll be versatile in their casting approach. Sometimes it works; sometimes it doesn't." She also helps her actors get a foothold in other markets, if that's what they're seeking. "We subscribe to

Breakdown Services, and if we see a role that one of our actors may be right for, I'll put a tape and resume in the mail and send it off to Los Angeles. We did that for *Richie Rich* a few years ago, and our client got the job. He was the chubby kid who ate everything." She adds, "We all know that L.A. is the pinnacle of this business, and I'm always trying to get my clients a foot in the door. It's never easy, but it's possible to cast a gig in L.A. from Chicago."

It's a lot easier when Hollywood comes to Chicago, as was the case with *Richie Rich, The Negotiator,* and *U.S. Marshalls.* Sa-Rah was also involved in casting day players for *Early Edition* and *Cupid.* Being persistent, says Conard, is the key to gaining attention from casting directors. "They don't have time to 'do lunch,'" she says. "We have to be creative. We send them photos of new talent, so they know we exist. It doesn't hurt for actors to drop [casting directors] a card every now and then, too, but it's primarily up to us to do the pitching." Conard makes sure every casting director knows when a client is starring in a stage play. "We don't rely much on videotape in Chicago," she explains. "They'd rather see actors perform live, unless we're talking about commercial talent, in which case the casting directors will want to see some examples on tape." She also says it's more important that an actor be good than good looking. "Beauty is only in the eye of the beholder, anyway. It definitely boils down to talent."

Conard is impatient with actors who refuse to take direction or want to take shortcuts. "For instance, don't have a friend take a black-and-white picture; spend a few dollars to hire a professional photographer." She's also looking for someone with a down-to-earth attitude. "When we meet someone with an inflated ego, we tell them straight away that we're not the agency for them. We just don't have the time or energy to feed egos." If an actor seems grounded, the agency will request a prepared monologue and then supply cold copy to assess his or her ability to be spontaneous. "I really like it when actors ask intelligent questions. It tells me they're serious and know what they want. I also enjoy sharing information with them, because if we're going to work together, it's best if each of us knows where the other's coming from instead of simply assuming. I tell people never to assume in this business." Conard encourages her actors to keep from being discouraged. "I feel this business is a numbers game," she says. "You have to remain persistent and professional. Eventually you knock on enough doors, and you're bound to open one or two. Once it opens, your career can skyrocket—if you're ready."

Nancy Curtis

HARDEN-CURTIS ASSOCIATES
850 Seventh Avenue, #405
New York, NY 10019
(212) 977-8502
FAX (212) 977-8420
HCAssc@aol.com

Nancy Curtis worked her way up the agent ladder from front-desk person to assistant agent to agent and then to partner in her own firm. After working together for years at another agency, Curtis and her partner, Mary Harden, realized they shared a common view of the business: a high regard for talent and the desire to work with clients who are ambitious and self-motivated. So in 1996 they formed Harden-Curtis Associates, a New York agency that handles actors in theater, film, and television. Harden splits her time between writers and actors. "We talk to producers on several levels, both selling talent and providing writers. It's a symbiotic relationship. We've found that these connections provide us with early access to projects in the developmental stage. It benefits us and all our clients."

They also have ten affiliates in Los Angeles and work with them on a regular basis. The New York office includes two young agents who've recently been promoted from assistants, Diane Riley and Michael Kirsten. "I'm a firm believer that home grown is good," says Curtis on her philosophy of promoting from within. "What's really nice about developing younger agents is that they remind you to be excited again. Their excitement about booking their first job or national tour, even just going to an opening, is contagious. I think the worst thing you can become in this business is jaded. You need to find a way to relive that great moment."

The staff at Harden-Curtis works as a team. Staff meetings are held on a continual basis, and everyone's opinion is valued. "I want their input," Curtis stresses. "I want to know why an agent would do something his or her way. What I appreciate about them is they'll ask me question after question, and they make me formulate ideas that I probably wouldn't have thought about, such as how I book pilots or what I look for in an actor." And what does Curtis look for when submitting for daytime and prime time? "Daytime is much more about the look," she believes. "It's about selling romance. My partner's husband, Richard Harden, once said, 'Nancy, daytime is modern-day opera,' and I agree with him. I even told him I was going to steal his line!"

But no matter which medium, it's talent she's seeking. "Talent is the most important thing, the first thing I look for in an actor." There's also the likeability factor. "Do you treat the front-desk person as nicely as you treat me? If not, I'm not interested. I also look for leaders who are presidents of their company. Look at the Kevin Costners or Tom Cruises; they understand that they're running a company, and they have to motivate their employees. I look for someone who knows how to motivate me, knows how to bring us all together, how to communicate and make his or her wishes known." She's attracted to actors who know how to get out there and shine. "I find that people who do the best know how to go after a showcase I may not have access to, get involved, get good reviews, and then let me handle the promotion. My job is getting the casting directors there, to talk up the show and get my clients seen. I want them to see us as the team, not just me as the team."

An example of teamwork is her relationship with Bruce Norris, who was offered a day's work on the feature *Parent Trap*. As so often happens with actors, he was offered another role that would conflict with the film, a role in a theatrical production at the prestigious Playwright's Horizons. "I said to him, 'Don't take the movie. Trust me. Twenty-five casting directors will see you in this show.' What happened was he listened to me, and one of those in the audience was Scott Rudin, who ended up casting him as a lead in *A Civil Action* with John Travolta. It was the nicest moment of the entire year."

Curtis finds her clients primarily through referrals. She also attends plays on a regular basis. She recommends that actors do whatever they can to get a friend or someone who believes in them to refer them to an agent. "I would see anyone referred to me by a casting director in this city, although that doesn't mean I'd automatically sign that person. He or she would have to back up the referral with great work." Once she does sign someone, Curtis is a dedicated promoter. When she represented Brett Butler, she was always running from club to club to see her perform. "She has so much talent. I would walk away, and my cheeks would be hurting from laughing so hard. I tried to tell casting directors what a great actress she was, but they only thought of her in terms of standup. When I finally convinced them to see her, they were always pleasantly surprised."

Curtis seeks a real symbiotic relationship. She hopes her client is going to follow her suggestions, and she always listens to what her client is saying. If the actor is looking for a television series in Los Angeles, Curtis is on the phone trying to get him or her in to see the casting director. "I'll call Mark Saks [Vice President of Talent and Casting for CBS Productions] and say, 'Mark, I heard about this great part, what about this client?' and he'll say, 'Can the person get here or can you put him or her on tape?'"

What is important to Curtis is what is important to the actor. "What is it that you want to accomplish, and how can I help you do that?" She has had clients meet visiting Los Angeles casting directors in her office in New York. She'll set up appointments with several of her clients or make sure the casting directors have tickets to the shows her clients are in. All she asks of clients is to do their best and maintain a positive attitude. "Your job as an actor is to learn how to deal with people. Your job is to inspire people." She also suggests a truth mirror, "which means you must be willing to hear what you may not want to hear. Get people to tell you the painful stuff so that you can turn around and try to fix it."

You may not agree with every bit of criticism that comes your way, but it shouldn't throw you into a fit of depression. Curtis recalls a client phoning her to find out why he didn't book a soap he had just auditioned for. "They said he was losing his hair, and that's why they didn't want him. Well, Bruce Willis is doing fine today, thank you very much, and a big part of that success is due to his attitude. The first thing out of his mouth was, 'You know, Nancy, that was really nice of you to find out for me. Thank you very much.' I remember hanging up the phone thinking this guy is going to be really successful. That guy knows how to run his own company."

Jeff Danis

INTERNATIONAL
CREATIVE MANAGEMENT
8942 Wilshire Boulevard
Beverly Hills, CA 90211
(310) 550-4304
FAX (310) 550-4490

When he began working as an agent, Jeff Danis had no idea that it would indeed become a career. "I just got a job at a top commercial agency in New York right after college, not knowing anything beyond that." But at the J. Michael Bloom talent agency, Danis received the best training possible to rise quickly through the ranks. "I was in New York during the heyday of commercials on the East Coast. I got a job as a commercial casting director at Grey Advertising, but when the business started heading west, so did I. It turned out to be the best thing I ever did, because I got into voice-overs, which I enjoy a lot more than on-camera."

Danis prefers representing voice-over actors for several reasons. "One is the clients. You have fewer, which I like. Two is that voice actors have a lot more longevity as high earners than on-camera commercial actors; a top voice client can make six or seven figures for up to thirty years. And three, as a voice-over agent you have more authority about who gets the jobs. As an on-camera agent, you just send your clients out and hope they get something. But I can help pinpoint actors and be more directly involved in their careers." Danis believes that if you're a well-respected agent in the voice-over field, you carry a lot of weight in the industry. And he does, as senior vice president for International Creative Management (ICM), one of the top talent agencies in the world.

The voice-over field has altered dramatically over the last ten years. "The most dramatic change is that everyone wants to be doing it. Years ago, when I began, the field was dominated by ten announcers, who were used over and over again. Today many great actors and every aspiring actor is doing voice-overs. Nowadays quirky is in, character is in, and often a non-sell approach is preferred. People who would never have had a career ten years ago now have highly established careers, because of the new trends." Danis has seen people literally taken off the street to become established voice-over artists. "A great story," he recalls, "concerns a gentleman I met a few years ago. He was a stadium announcer who was also a part-time manager of an apartment building in the San Fernando Valley. He had a very interesting and powerful voice but had not established himself in the field and didn't know how. I took him on, and during his first year he became the voice of a major network, and he hasn't stopped since." It was almost like winning the lottery. "If you have the right voice, you're in," Danis proclaims.

Of course, actors can always improve their chances of success by studying and by honing their skills. "I love improv classes," Danis admits. "It gives actors a certain rhythm to the voice, and they get a quickness to their pace." He also recommends other acting classes as well as a microphone technique class. "There are many wonderful actors who can't do voice-over, because they have no idea how to work a mike. They're used to props and costumes and camera angles, but they don't know when to pull their voice back and forth in front of the microphone or how to throw their voice or shade their voice. These are specific techniques that have to be learned." Danis suggests studying voice technique with one of the top voice casting directors, since they're the ones tapped into the industry and can impart the latest knowledge to their students.

Danis is always on the prowl for new clients, whether they're performing in showcases, theater, or even more unusual presentations. "One of my classic stories is how I found E. G. Daily, the voice of the pig in *Babe* and Tommy Pickles in *Rugrats*. I found her in a wrestling show at the Roxy fifteen years ago. She was portraying a wrestler, but her voice was unique. She had acting experience but had never done any voice-over work." Danis was attracted to her raspy quality, which lends itself to playing young characters. The late Dana Hill is another example of a voice discovery. "I saw her in *Picnic* at the Ahmanson Theatre, and although she was an established actress, voice-overs were new to her. She became the voice on many very hot cartoon series, including *Peter Pan*. Even when her on-camera career wasn't flourishing, she had the voice work to keep her going." Today, not only are film and theater actors turning to voice-overs, but many top celebrities are lending their voices to animated features, making it all the more difficult for veteran voice actors to compete. "It's fun work for them, and it's also a nice legacy for their children."

Danis is fortunate to be one of the first agents a producer will call when seeking talent. "They'll tell me what they're looking for and have us hold the audition either in our office or at their facility. The beauty of Los Angeles is that most of the country comes here for their voices, because they feel we have the best talent pool. New York used to have the majority of the business, but today Los Angeles has become a mecca for voice-overs." Another option is having clients audition at a voice casting facility, which acts as the middleman for agents and ad agencies. Of course, the best scenario is when a producer has no time for a casting session and simply asks Danis to suggest an actor to fit the bill. "Then we discuss names, and we come to an agreement and book the job over the phone."

Ten to twenty voices are typically included on a submission tape. Danis explains that when an actor doesn't land the spot, it's because most producers will go to four or five agencies looking for talent, which means that perhaps the client is one of sixty voices being considered. "When my client asks, 'Why didn't I get that commercial?' I answer, 'Because someone else did.' The reality is that they only need one voice, and most of those submitted were probably very good and could have done the job. It's someone else's turn now. Tomorrow maybe it'll be yours."

Danis suggests a path to achieve success: Be creative. "You're not just the hired help," Danis explains. "You're there to be a teacher in many ways. If you have some creative ideas and can improvise, they respect that. You shouldn't just go in and read the words and leave. You're part of the process. They like input. If they wanted someone just to read what's on the page, they'd hire their families. They want you, because you can bring something more to it. You can help sell it."

Some further words of advice from this respected voice-over agent: "If you're willing to go the extra mile; if you're willing to be flexible and willing to run around town when the calls come in, you'll be way out front. You have to be receptive and willing to play the game, to go the extra mile. We are very lucky to be given the chance to be in this field," he stresses. "Never lose your perspective. Realize that this is a gift and make the most of it."

Robin Dornbaum

JORDAN, GILL AND
DORNBAUM AGENCY, INC.
156 Fifth Avenue, #711
New York, NY 1001
(212) 463-8455
FAX (212) 691-6111

When Robin Dornbaum was attending college, she was offered an internship at a commercial casting office and found herself fascinated with those folks behind the scenes. "I thought it was more interesting to find out who was sending the actors to us than sitting in the room every day, watching actors delivering the same lines over and over again." And so, when she graduated the following year, she turned to the agent business, where she has been ever since. These days, Dornbaum is one of the partners of a major children's agency in New York that handles over one hundred actors from infants to young adults.

Dornbaum works primarily with her signed clients, but also freelances with managers' clients. "I work with ten or twelve children's managers, which gives me access to hundreds of other kids." For example, a casting director may want to see ten kids of a certain type for a commercial. I may only have three or four of that type signed to me, so I call on managers' kids who are right for the spot and send them along on the audition. We'll freelance children for commercials; however, for legit or theatrical, the agency will only send out our signed clients, since we're interested in building their careers."

"The difference between kids in Los Angeles and New York," she explains, "is that here kids primarily consider acting an after-school activity. It isn't the focus of their lives, whereas in L.A., it's a career. It seems to me that kids here in New York tend to be more well-rounded. After-school activities like sports and hobbies are encouraged. In L.A., kids don't always have time for that if they're going on auditions every day. We also don't have as much work as in L.A. New York probably gets more commercial work, but there are more legit opportunities in Los Angeles." They groom their clients to go to Los Angeles for pilot season, because they believe they have a better chance of booking there. "We have relationships with some great agencies there that really support our clients, such as Coast to Coast, Judy Savage, and Osbrink Talent."

While Los Angeles has a bunch of agencies solely representing children, Jordan, Gill and Dornbaum is it in New York. "Children and children," says Dornbaum. "And, just as in life, some ages are better than others for the business." Babies, she explains, tend to work a great deal until they reach twenty-four months. "Then the terrible twos hit, and even though your offspring might be an angel, the reputation of a two-year-old precedes the child. You can stand on your head, but a two-year-old who doesn't want to perform simply won't do it." Most children, she adds, start working actively when they're three and a half to six. "That's when they're at their cutest, and they can also listen to, and follow, directions. When they hit six or seven their teeth fall out, and they are more self-conscious. Most commercials want good teeth, especially ones that are promoting food products." Kids apparently regain their foothold in the commercial world at age eight and continue strong until they hit puberty. "The braces come on, the voices are changing, and the girls are growing every which way. This is the hardest age for commercial kids," she emphasizes, "because they're just changing too much." Once they're sixteen, they're back in the game, because so many commercials focus on that age. Of course, as most agents agree, if you're older and can play younger, you're much more in demand. "Emily Young, the Welch's girl, is one of our clients. She looked like a four-year-old when she was six, so she blew the four-year-olds away because of her maturity and understanding."

When it comes to stage actors, it's a little different. The kids, she says, are more committed to their craft. They take dance and vocal classes and study acting. Dornbaum doesn't believe that kids under twelve need to really study acting, especially if they're only doing commercials. She prefers the natural quality of young children. In fact, they take on lots of kids who've never acted a day in their lives. "I'm looking for kids who have great personalities and high energy and can react more than act. I also look for really smart kids, because they tend to be good readers and can understand scripts better. We're the kind of agency that takes a kid and really develops and markets him or her." If the child is enthusiastic and the parent is nice, it's a winning combination. "We don't often see 'stage moms' in New York. Parents here tend not to be as obsessive and crazy about the business. In fact, my clients often grow up and put their own kids in the business, since they themselves had such positive experiences. Remember Mikey from the Life cereal commercials?" she asks. "We represented him, and now we represent his children."

Dornbaum loves having her clients call to say they've just paid for their college education or bought their first car or house from the money they earned on jobs as kids. Other clients have amazing experiences while on the job. "I just had a kid book a Merrill Lynch commercial for which she got to go to Germany, South Africa, and China for almost a month; and another client just got back from New Zealand, where he shot a commercial. I'm sending a five-year-old girl tomorrow to Yugoslavia for a month to film a movie. That's what makes this business so exciting," she admits. But no matter how much she believes in a client, if that child starts acting up and complaining about the time and effort spent on auditions, she encourages parents to pull out for a while. "Some of these kids have to drive hours after school to get to an audition. Parents need to know when it's getting to be too much. You never want children to stop being children. If it's not the focus of their lives, they tend to appreciate it more. This is a very positive business, as long as you go in and have fun. That's what it should be about for kids. It shouldn't be a job. It should be a fun experience."

Mary Anne Duffy

NEAL HAMIL AGENCY
7887 San Felipe, #227
Houston, TX 77063
(713) 789-1335
FAX (713) 789-6163

It all started in 1974 when Mary Anne Duffy's husband, who worked for a film company in Houston, called her and asked if she could find twenty people for a bank commercial. "At the time I was raising our two boys and serving as the president of the Ladies' Club. I pulled twenty friends together, and we did that commercial, as well as several others. It was fun, but we weren't getting paid." So she decided to have a local photographer take pictures of her and the other ladies, which she then compiled into a portfolio. "I started calling on all the ad agencies and photo studios in town, and soon became the first talent agent in Houston."

After undergoing both knee and hip replacements, Duffy found she could no longer run her own agency, and she decided to work for someone else. She has been teamed with Neal Hamil for about two years. Together they handle close to two hundred actors, both adults and children, for on-camera, print, and voice-over work. Some of her former clients include John Jackson of *Jag,* Tracy Scoggins of *Babylon 5,* and Joan Severance of *The Love Boat.* Most of the work for which she submits is out of Dallas and includes commercials, magazine and newspaper ads, billboards, radio, educational and training films, calendars, and conventions. "Most of our calls are for commercials," she admits. "That's our strongest area. In Houston itself, there's more commercial work available than film." But when it comes to industrials, Duffy also gets calls from outside the state. "We're always pursuing clients," she explains. "We'll call the Texas Film Commission to get lists of current projects in production. We're forever sending mailers, pictures, and resumes. We also subscribe to Breakdown Services in Los Angeles and maintain friendly relationships with casting directors there."

Duffy tries not to handle too many actors at one time. "Generally when a job comes in there are just a few of our clients who fit the specs. I like to have ten to fifteen actors who don't look the same in each of the age ranges or categories. For example, it's not good to have ten blondes who look alike or are about the same age. Ten actors who are appropriate, but different, give the producers more variety from which to choose." An actor's look is important, but that doesn't mean that the look has to be drop-dead gorgeous. "The look should be different; not average or beauty queen, but rather someone with a twinkle in the eyes, something special that makes the person glow. If you have that look, it's easy to get representation."

Duffy will represent an actor for a six-month trial period. By the end of that period, if the actor doesn't work out, she'll ask him or her to look elsewhere. "Why waste time with someone who refuses to continue training or keep current on their photos and resumes? If an actor isn't getting auditions after that length of time, it's a waste of both our times."

A good headshot and resume are vital to Duffy. In fact, she asks actors for two headshots, one serious and one with a smile. "One should be casual and the other more dressy. The headshot shouldn't be too dark or too light, and the eyes have got to sparkle." She'll help her clients select the appropriate shots from the proof sheet. "We also have a sample resume we'd like our talent to follow. It should show the theater you've done and the roles you've gotten in film, TV, and industrials. It should be condensed to a single page with the most current work first." If an actor doesn't have a lot of credits, Duffy suggests doing as much theater as possible, as well as studying with a good coach. "An actor should never stop taking lessons. Some actors think they're naturals who don't need to do anything, but look at today's superstars. They're still taking classes." For those actors who aren't used to the discipline of film or television, she also recommends doing work as extras.

Self-marketing is something the Neal Hamil Agency promotes. "An actor should do as much of that as possible. Send postcards to let producers and casting directors know what you've been doing. Put together a good videotape of your commercial and dramatic work so that when we're working with out-of-state clients, we can show them what you can do." That, to Duffy, is being professional. What is not professional, and what she cannot abide, is the actor who crashes an audition without an appointment or someone who forgets a headshot or, even worse, the audition itself. "I've had talent miss auditions because they never checked their answering machines. Every actor should have a pager," she insists. "That's the only way to be available at all times." She also prefers that an actor use a map rather than call a casting director or producer for directions. She feels it's part of the actor's responsibility.

Duffy knows what it takes for success and tries to enlighten her actors with her knowledge. "I definitely believe that what goes around comes around. I think people with good personalities who are cooperative are the ones who make it in this line of business. They must be able to communicate effectively and keep a healthy mental attitude despite all the rejection they face." She knows it isn't easy, and while her job isn't always easy either, there's nothing Duffy enjoys more than being an agent. "If there's such a thing as a next life, I hope I'll be an agent in that one, too," she quips. "I can't think of anything I'd rather do. I love telling people they got the job. I stay in this business because I love people. You can bet I'll never retire."

Karen Forman

METROPOLITAN TALENT AGENCY
4526 Wilshire Boulevard
Los Angeles, CA 90010
(213) 857-4595
FAX (213) 857-4599

Metropolitan Talent is housed in a wonderful turn-of-the-century mansion in the nostalgic Wilshire District of Los Angeles. No modern sculptures or issues of fashion magazines adorn this waiting room; nervous actors awaiting interviews can soothe their nerves by looking at early American collectibles and art journals. It's definitely a more personal environment than many similar agencies, and that's one of the reasons Karen Forman opted for Metropolitan. After graduating from college she worked for three and a half years at CAA (Creative Artists Agency). Three years ago she was promoted to head of talent at Metropolitan, along with Adam Levine.

Metropolitan boasts fourteen agents and considers itself midsize. "We're an alternative agency," Forman explains. "We represent 125 carefully chosen actors, and we work very closely with each one. We don't have hundreds of actors with not enough agents to service them. We also don't believe in signing a lot of actors right before pilot season to bulk up our list to submit to casting directors. We focus on careers."

All agents work together for the individual client. "When we sign someone, all of us have to agree. It's the only thing we ever really fight over," she admits. The agents divide their chores according to studio and network. For instance, if Forman is responsible for Universal features, she has to know all the projects going on at that studio so that her clients will be able to get a shot at any opportunity that may become available. "Our motto is 'We work for the people we have.' If we do a good job, others will come our way because of our reputation."

Metropolitan's clients do get work; 75 percent work consistently, including Jane Seymour, James Brolin, and Cloris Leachman. However, even those with less name recognition go out on a lot of auditions. Forman and the other agents at Metropolitan are patient. If an actor doesn't make it big after a few years but the feedback from casting directors has been good, the agency will continue to work hard for the person. But it's tough when work is slow and actors don't go out for months at a time. "I try at least to set up general meetings so that they don't get completely frustrated. I talk to them and let them know it's not them, it's the business. The one thing I learned at CAA," Forman stresses, "is that we have to return everyone's phone calls the same day. If you don't call them back right away, they may be running a network tomorrow, and they'll remember."

Despite the number of actors it handles, Metropolitan is careful to avoid conflicts; the agency won't sign someone in a certain category if that category is full. It's quality versus quantity, which translates into a lot of unsolicited submissions being rejected on a daily basis. "The first thing I tell actors when I lecture at schools is not to send me a picture and resume, because it's a waste of money. I won't look at them unless someone has called me on the phone and advised me to be on the lookout for it." Referrals are respected and taken into consideration, even if they're out of the ordinary. "We had never represented kids, but a manager insisted we see a young comedian who was special. He had no experience. He was seventeen. We went to see him perform out of respect for the manager. There was something charismatic about him, and I convinced the agents to consider him. They all agreed, so we took a chance on him. Now, Nick Cannon has an overall deal with Will Smith's company to develop a series in which he'll star for Nickelodeon."

Those on whom Metropolitan won't take a chance are actors too set in a specific character. "About a year ago a great-looking guy in his early twenties came in to meet with me. The problem was his image. He was a Johnny Depp wannabe with messy hair and gold chains. I couldn't get past his look. If he had tape of five or six different characters he could play, that would have been different, but I passed on him."

The hottest category in television and film today, says Forman, is the sixteen- to twenty-four-year-old attractive actor. The next most popular, and harder to find, is the handsome thirty- to forty-year-old leading man with credits. "And if you're able to do comedy on top of that, you can get into any agency!"

In order for Forman and the other agents at Metropolitan to sell an actor, they need to know what they're selling. If an actor wants an agent to push a career, it's imperative that the agent be excited about the actor's talent. Having a good tape is important, unless you're just out of school. "What are we going to talk about during our meeting if we haven't seen what you're capable of doing? I met a young actress the other day who was referred by a manager. She was very sweet, but we had nothing to discuss because she didn't have tape. I need to get a feel for who you are and what roles you can play." Forman won't look at prepared scenes. "We used to, and it was very uncomfortable for us. It only shows you can memorize something, but it doesn't show your range or how you look on camera."

Feedback following an audition is important for both the agent and the actor. "The writers may have changed the look or age of the character, and if I don't call, I won't know that. I have to talk to the casting director and give my actor the best shot." That also applies to going against type. If there's a listing in Breakdown Services for a tall, blonde actress in her thirties, Forman may submit a black or

Hispanic actress or even a male if it would be appropriate to the script. "If we sat around waiting for roles written just for minorities, I'd have a lot of unhappy clients not going out on many auditions."

The most difficult aspect of Forman's job, she admits, is building a career, only to have the actor wooed away by another agency. "What troubles me most is that it's not always in the actor's best interest to be with a larger agency. But that's what happens all the time. It becomes an issue about the size or status of the agency rather than the actor. At least I know when they leave it's because we've done an amazing job or the larger agents wouldn't be interested. So if we lose actors because we're doing our job, I guess if they're going to go, that's the way to go."

Carol Freed

STELLAR MODEL AND
TALENT AGENCY
407 Lincoln Road, #2K
Miami Beach, FL 32139
(305) 672-2217
FAX (305) 672-2365
stlrtalent@aol.com

Early in life, Carol Freed was faced with a dilemma. Here was a young woman with a bachelor's degree in criminal justice, but in order to continue on that path, she would have to apply to law school, and she wasn't sure if she really wanted that. Then her mother-in-law offered her a proposition: If Freed would learn the business, she could one day take over Stellar Model and Talent. "I was getting fed up with school," she recalls. "This would be something that would someday be my very own, so I decided to accept her proposal. I liked it a lot."

Freed has been an agent now for six years. Stellar Model and Talent has three full-time agents handling theatrical, print, commercial, voice-over, and children, representing actors of all ethnicities, especially Hispanics, since there's a large population of Latinos in the area. "We have several advertising agencies in Miami that specialize in Latin commercials. There are also three TV stations that broadcast in Spanish. They produce series, novellas, and commercials and cast here as well as elsewhere." Although Stellar is a union-franchised agency and most of the television and film with which it's involved is union, Hispanic television is nonunion.

Actors are handled either exclusively or nonexclusively, depending on the situation. "Most actors would like to be exclusive with us," says Freed. "They know we'll work harder for them, and they won't have to deal with 'beeper wars,' checking in with lots of different agents every day to see if there's work. It's easy to fall through the cracks if you're not signed with an agent. But we won't sign every actor. If an actor doesn't have a lot of experience, and we want to see if we can get the person work, we'll submit him or her for various projects and see the response." Casting directors in cities other than Los Angeles are used to having actors submitted by a variety of agents. It's especially common for young actors just starting out, who still need to amass a number of credits before an agent will be comfortable signing them.

When seeking talent for its roster, Stellar looks for experience. "I want to see that an actor isn't merely an extra. We want actors who've had speaking parts in film and have been principals in commercials. If they've primarily done theater, we want them to have had the lead or at least a supporting role on stage. Those are the actors we want to sign on an exclusive basis."

Most of the submissions they receive are unsolicited. Some are referred by friends or casting directors. When Freed is interested in meeting an actor she'll set up an interview. "I won't read an actor. I'm not an expert in judging a monologue, but if an actor has tape, I'll see how he or she looks on camera. That's important, but having a tape is not critical. I'm more interested in how they come across at an interview."

Freed recommends that her clients either take classes at the Actors' Conservatory or study with Stuart Solomon, who teaches film, commercial, and voice-over technique in town. "Some of our models have never been on camera, and they especially need to take classes to learn to deliver lines." Of course, when seeking models, beauty is important, but for television and film, Freed looks for character types as well as perfect features. And photographs are critical. "I'll give my clients a list of photographers I think are the most professional. They can choose which ones they prefer. Models and children need composites, but for TV and film we rely on simple headshots." What bothers Freed most is the actor who shows up at an audition without a headshot. "That's just not professional," she insists. "That's as bad as not showing up at a casting session without calling. If [the actors] call first, we can usually get them seen at another time. A client often holds a callback, and we can reschedule the actor for that session, but if [actors] just don't show up, they lose out, and it makes us look bad, too."

The agency has been in business for ten years in Miami Beach and has a good reputation. The agents don't just submit their actors for local projects; they also subscribe to Breakdown Services in New York and often get calls from casting directors back east. "One of our Hispanic actors wanted to go to New York, so we submitted him on tape for *One Life to Live* and he got it. He worked the soap for a year and a half." Other success stories include Monica Potter, who was cast in Los Angeles on *The Young and the Restless* and went on to star in *Con Air* and *Patch Adams*. "I'd really love to see more of my clients go on to New York and L.A. It's very exciting for us all," Freed declares. And if an actor leaves for a major East or West Coast talent office, so be it. She understands that that's the nature of the business. What she doesn't understand is why an actor would need a manager in Miami Beach. "I also don't think an actor needs to spend hundreds of dollars on a service that charges them for photographs and agency lists. If an actor wants photographs, look [photographers] up in the phone book! And the local SAG office has a list of franchised agents in the area. Why spend money for it?"

Freed hopes actors develop a professional attitude as they learn their craft. "It's so important to be prepared and responsible. Without those attributes, you'll fail. When you have an audition, you should go in with the thought that you're going to get the job. Be prepared to give them what they want, even if they don't know what they want, which is often the case until they see it. Perhaps you're not what they originally had in mind, so change their mind. You can do it with the right attitude. You're an actor, aren't you?"

Martin Gage

THE GAGE GROUP
9255 Sunset Boulevard, #515
Los Angeles, CA 90069
(310) 859-8777

A visit with Martin Gage is a virtual retrospective of showbiz in perhaps its most glamorous, certainly its most memorable era. This veteran of Hollywood agents has been in the business for more than thirty years and still loves to reminisce about his days on the stage. Photos of Gage as a handsome young actor are prominently displayed for visitors to admire. Ask him about his earlier career and he'll gladly tell you all about his tap dancing on radio to "Sunny Side of the Street" and his close friendship with Sal Mineo and Valerie Harper. Some of his current clients, in fact, are former buddies from New York's famed Studio One. So how did Gage make the transition from actor to actor's rep? Let's say it was an accident. Literally.

Gage was leaving his final callback for *West Side Story* in 1956. He was crossing Broadway and 45th Street when he was hit by a taxi. "Smashed to pieces. A month later, my agent came to see me in the hospital and whispered in my ear that I got the role of Baby John." Well, I was happy to hear it, but I certainly couldn't do it. I couldn't work for two years. But to tell you the truth, I probably would have gotten fired if I had accepted the role. I really wasn't a dancer. I faked it. Even my acting. I took classes from an old Russian teacher who once asked me if I had learned anything from her. I told her if I ever had to play an old Russian countess, I'd be great!" Gage admits he simply didn't want to put the effort into real training, so he decided to get a job with an agent as a trainee. "After about a year I decided to open my own office, since I knew practically everyone in the business anyway. I starved to death."

Gage accepted a position installing a legit department at the Fifi Oscard commercial agency. "The first year I got Broadway roles for forty-two actors. I loved it. It wasn't until that moment that I decided to stay. I even stopped dyeing my hair." One of his first finds was Bernadette Peters. "I saw her perform in summer stock. In two years she was a star." Another find was a young man who was working in the chorus of a New York show. Paul Sorvino signed with Gage, and he has been working ever since. Soon the Oscard Agency became Oscard-Gage Ltd., and following that, Gage decided it was time to go solo. In 1973, he opened the Gage Group and expanded his business to Los Angeles two years later.

He much prefers working for himself. "I don't have a corporate mentality," he says proudly. "I won't play those games. I don't do lunches. I don't like closed doors.

I start working at home at 7:30 in the morning. I sit in my old ratty bathrobe. I keep getting beautiful robes from clients, but I never wear them. When everyone is doing lunch, I'm taking a shower. When one of my clients asks why I won't do lunch, I answer, 'If you want to fire me as your agent, do it in the office. Not over lunch. I have enough indigestion as it is.'"

Gage is still in love with theater. "I have actors who come from New York and start to pick up bad tricks working in TV. I finally tell them to go back to New York and do a play." If one of his clients wants to do theater, he'll suggest Seattle, South Coast Repertory in Orange County, or the Old Globe in San Diego rather than Los Angeles. He has always found a great many clients through theater. He recalls finally meeting one of his favorite women of the stage, Geraldine Page, in New York. A casting director friend, Gary Shaffer, had invited him to see her on Broadway. "We went backstage and I was thrilled, even though she was kind of frumpy. She only cared about her art." Page had representation in Los Angeles but was getting only bit parts. "When she told her agent she was going to do *Ghosts,* he asked her if it was a horror movie. She told him it was the Henrik Ibsen play. He said, 'I didn't know Henry Gibson wrote plays!'"

When Page realized Gage knew who Ibsen was, she was relieved. "She said, 'Ooh, a Hollywood agent who knows about Ibsen. Okay, I'll come with you.' I called people in town to tell them I had signed Geraldine Page and they'd say, 'So?' I just kept banging on doors, begging them just to look at her tape. I'd promise them a wrist corsage if she got the job. Well, not only did she get a job, she got an Emmy nomination and won an Oscar for *Trip to Bountiful.* She never left me, until she died." Gage learned a lot from his favorite client. "Geraldine was asked to do a small role in *The Pope of Greenwich Village,* and I discouraged her from doing the three-page scene. She loved the role and told me if they put the camera on her, she'd really know what to do with that character. I listened and realized I didn't know it all." Page received another Academy Award nomination for that part.

Gage's belief in his clients has gained him a great deal of respect in Hollywood. "When I first came up with Kim Basinger, they said, 'Who?' I told them she was a model from New York. 'A model? Can she talk?' Or Halle Berry. I knew she was gonna be a star. There was not one beautiful young African-American star at that time. She came out here, and we put her in a series right away. The series was awful, but it didn't take long to get her into film." And while Gage is thrilled to have his clients starring in a series, as soon as pilot season ends, he hopes to have his actors on a plane to New York. "That's where an actor sharpens his skills, especially when you've been on a series where you learn lots of tricks and shortcuts. Stage is about discipline."

He suggests actors put together a great demo reel. "It used to be you could get by with a photo and resume. Now it's tape. I tape all the TV shows my clients are in so that I can see the billing and the scene, but I hate watching television." Gage had always fought against online casting, too, because he feared it would remove the agent from the process, but he now realizes it's the future and has come to accept it. And everyone accepts him, even though he can be a tough negotiator. "I can get just about anybody on the phone," he boasts, then adds, "It's probably because I'm so old, they feel they have to. They yell at me for talking them into doling out more money for my clients, but then I tell them an off-color joke, and they wind up laughing and feeling better about the whole thing. Why become enemies over it?" Gage's dream is to build a career on which he can retire some day, and he claims his biggest fear is still that "Someone's going to find out I'm faking it!"

Abby Girvin

DOROTHY DAY OTIS PARTNERS
215 South La Cienega Boulevard, PH
Beverly Hills, CA 90211
(310) 289-8011
FAX (310) 289-8136
www.ddoagency.com

Ever since she can remember, Abby Girvin has wanted to be in Los Angeles. After graduating from college she decided to form a high-fashion agency for young models in Washington, D.C. "I used to visit San Diego every summer, and I knew that someday I'd be on the West Coast." Nearly four years ago she made the move and became an agent with Dorothy Day Otis, a full-service agency featuring on-camera, print, children's, and one of the best dance departments in Los Angeles. Girvin's area of expertise is adult commercials. "We handle about two hundred actors in our commercial department. Thirty percent work consistently, making a living from doing commercials."

The agency prefers actors with a strong professional background but will take on those with less experience if they have an interesting look or are extremely talented in a specific area. "I found a lady in her late seventies, a ballerina. A friend had told me I had to meet her. She assured me she had something special to offer, a certain sparkle. Well, she has booked about a dozen commercials over the last year, and she has never taken a commercial class! People just want to be around her; she has such vitality and energy." Another elderly client booked a commercial on his first audition and is now doing billboards and other print campaigns. He was referred to her through a casting director. "This client can't really act, but he goes in and is himself, which I believe is the most important thing."

Most of the meetings with new actors come from referrals, Girvin explains. "We love referrals, whether they come from casting directors or clients who work a lot. If a casting director tells me there's an actor I must see, I'll always set up a meeting. Then it's up to the actor to perform." She usually provides the talent with ten choices of commercial copy, from which she asks the actor to select two pieces of different styles. "I like them to choose one that's a little quirky and one that's more down to earth to get an idea of what they can do. I also ask them what kinds of commercials they've done in the past and if they have relationships with casting directors." Girvin also likes to see where actors are studying. "Even if they have a lot of experience behind them, classes open their eyes to other things. For instance, commercials can very subtly change with the times. It's a good idea to take a brush-up course every so often to make sure you're keeping up with the trends." Classes, she believes, teach actors to be themselves and be real. "It teaches you to trust in yourself, which is very important, especially at an audition."

Headshots are another critical ingredient for an actor's portfolio. "It's in the eyes. They have to be crystal clear. Don't retouch them too much. They have to look like you. You only have a second to reach a casting director. That's why it's so important to have a great photo." The same holds true if you're looking for an agent. She recommends getting referrals from casting directors. "It's the best way to get your foot in the door. If you are new to the business, a mass mailing is another option. But be creative," she insists. "I remember a girl sending us a head-shot from the neck down. She caught my attention, and we called her in. We also got a joint once, but I wouldn't recommend that." She pauses. "It was original, though." Another way to get an agent's attention is by taking a commercial work-shop that culminates with a showcase to which agents are invited. "I've taken on a lot of great people I've seen at showcases. It's a great way to find talent."

Girvin refers newcomers to the Actors' Network, an organization of over five hundred actors who can help people get started in the business through referrals. The Actors' Network holds meetings to which casting directors and other industry pros are invited. "They have notes on every agent, including me, I'm sure. I'm even scared to think what those notes contain," she quips. "If someone is new to the business, this is a great way to start." She also suggests that actors intern with an agent or casting director to gain insight and make connections. "You should do it for at least a couple of months, even if it's a half day a week. We currently repre-sent one of our interns, who has now been promoted to an assistant at the agency."

According to Girvin, the agency is very proactive. "We usually submit five choices for a specific job. I love it when we have to beg a casting director to see one of our clients and they end up booking the job. That tells us we know what we're doing." A few weeks ago, Girvin recalls a breakdown for an upscale New York female. "We pitched a lady who was against type—a risky way to go. They fell in love with her the minute she walked into the room, and she booked the job." That, of course, is what keeps Girvin riveted to her work. "I am a people person. I enjoy making people happy. What can be better than helping someone who's been trying for a long time to make it in this business succeed? I enjoy making dreams come true."

Geoffrey Goldstein

INNOVATIVE ARTISTS
1999 Avenue of the Stars, #2850
Los Angeles, CA 90067
(310) 553-5200
FAX (310) 557-2211

For Geoffrey Goldstein, being an agent is a fairly recent development. He has been in the business for more than eight years, but he has only been a franchised agent for five. And it wasn't something he'd planned to do when he emigrated from Miami, where he had been working in the business-equipment and greeting-card industries. He came out to Los Angeles with his friend Craig Shapiro, who immediately got a job as an agent. "I was so naive," Goldstein recalls. "I didn't even know actors needed agents to represent them. But after spending another year in greeting cards and becoming more fascinated with the entertainment business, I wanted to give it a shot." With Shapiro's help, Goldstein was able to get his foot in the door at the William Morris Agency—in the mailroom, naturally. He learned quickly, climbing the proverbial ladder and winding up at Innovative, where his friend had also come to roost.

Innovative has sixteen talent agents in Los Angeles, representing about 350 adult and young-adult actors. The agency works hard at helping their younger clients transition into the adult category. "Take Joseph Mazzello, for instance," says Goldstein. "He's fifteen and has appeared in *Simon Burch* and *Jurassic Park*. Both theatrical departments have been following up on him, making sure he doesn't fall through the cracks as he graduates to adult." Another crossover client is Jack Johnson, who portrayed Will Robinson in *Lost in Space*. "He's now eleven and is also a crossover actor who we're developing for more adult roles." Innovative prides itself on developing talent. "It's our company philosophy. We're not just into getting actors jobs; we're trying to build careers as well."

The agency works on a system of collective representation. All four hundred clients on both coasts are actually part of one list. "There are no 'separate' departments and no 'point' people. Each agent covers a separate list of casting people, and whatever projects those casting directors happen to be handling at the time, our agents will submit from our one list. We each cover a number of studios, too, where we gather information on what's coming up that might be appropriate for our talent." When covering the studios, Innovative agents often team with other departments, such as literary (which represents writers, directors, and producers) or below-the-line (which represents the high-end technical people such as editors and cinematographers), to make sure they're getting the most mileage they can. "We track what's happening at the studios internally on a state-of-the-art computer system, where we keep a five-thousand-page feature grid about what's happening at every studio. From the time a book sale is announced in the trades, it's entered into our computer and someone is assigned to follow up on it. While it may not get made for five years, we're tracking it the entire time."

Innovative also relies heavily on its e-mail system so that if a client isn't available at a particular time, all the agents in Los Angeles and New York will be apprised of that. "It wouldn't be very professional if we accepted an offer for a client, not knowing another agent has already accepted another offer. That can't happen with our system. Every agent is responsible for entering and updating this information. It's part of the job." Another part of the job is being persistent if you think a client is right for a particular job. Goldstein cites a perfect example: long-time client Lou Diamond Phillips. "The New York office had been pursuing the lead role in the revival of the *King and I* for Lou on Broadway. No one in their wildest dreams would have thought of him for that role, or thought anyone could successfully replace Yul Brynner. But we were successful, and Lou got a Tony nomination for the role."

At one point the agency also represented Jared Leto, who at the time was not a familiar name. "We had put him on the map by getting him on the series *My So Called Life* with Claire Danes, and he had also done some minor feature work. I remember one of our literary agents chatting with Hollywood Pictures one day, asking what they were working on. They mentioned *Pre*, about Steve Prefontaine, the '70s Olympic long-distance runner. We asked what the character was like, and when we got the specifics, we mentioned Jared. They gave us the script on the spot, and he got the lead." Leto is no longer a client, but Innovative is proud of having brought him the attention he deserved. "It's part of the business. Clients come and go. You have to understand that." And while clients may not always be loyal to the agency, the agency feels a responsibility to its clients, especially since all fourteen theatrical agents have to approve a new addition to the roster. "If four people aren't interested, and they have to cover a third of the industry, it wouldn't be fair. They wouldn't push the actor to the studios they're covering, and the actor wouldn't be fully represented. We all have to be passionate about our clients. They're counting on us. It's a system of democracy."

Most of Innovative's clients are strong, experienced actors, known entities who've done at least some independent films or a few pilots. "If you haven't been recommended, chances are you won't get an interview here," Goldstein admits. "If a manager suggests someone, we'll always see the person. We'll take a chance on a newcomer if the actor is referred, because we won't be taking the chance alone."

And most of those newcomers are young. "We have to consider age. If you're young and it doesn't work out, you can always go somewhere else; it's not a big deal. But if you're thirty or forty and it doesn't work out, that would be a lot harder to deal with." As for representing various ethnicities, the agency's door is always open. "There's no color barrier here," says Goldstein. "A role may be written for a Caucasian, but we'll submit all ethnicities, because an actor is an actor. Years ago one of our agents was working on *Star Trek: Deep Space Nine* when it was being cast. They were seeking the next William Shatner or Patrick Stewart. We represent Avery Brooks, who David Rose, one of our agents, kept pushing. He was finally persuasive enough to get them to think beyond the prototypical starship captain, and he booked it." .

Every piece of mail that comes across Goldstein's desk is opened. "I actually look at every submission, and I wind up getting a few clients that way. A manager once sent me a picture and demo tape of one of his clients, and I called back immediately and wound up signing the actor. She became a regular on the John Larroquette TV series *Payne*, the American version of the British *Fawlty Towers*." The bottom line is that if you have an interesting photo and resume, some good credits, and someone who believes in you enough to make the referral, Innovative will be happy to consider you. And if you're lucky enough to be one of those selected, you'll have a dedicated team of professionals in your court, more than willing to take you from struggling newcomer to accomplished actor. As Goldstein professes, "We'll help you make the metamorphosis from caterpillar to butterfly."

Frank Gonzales

THE AGENCY
1800 Avenue of the Stars, #400
Los Angeles, CA 90067
(310) 551-3000
FAX (310) 551-1424

A relative newcomer to the business of agenting, Frank Gonzales has only been on the job a little over five years, and it wasn't something he had planned when he was a student in college. "I actually majored in economics," he admits. "All I knew when I graduated was that I wanted an easy job." He worked at Fox as a page. His outgoing personality led him into networking with actors and directors, and he was given an opportunity at The Agency in the mailroom. Within a few months, he was at a desk. "Up until only a year ago, I hadn't even been able to sign actors. I was aiding other agents with their clients. Now I can finally tell actors myself that we'd like to have them on board."

The Agency has traditionally been conservative but has started moving toward a younger clientele. "It's a youth market. A thirteen-year-old with a few credits and a lot of spark could get my attention. A thirty-year-old looking for representation would have to be more established." And they're usually referrals. "I won't see unsolicited actors," he says, "although my boss, Jerry Zeitman, thinks we all should consider photos and resumes that come across our desks. Jerry goes through every single one. In fact, one of these unsolicited actors was just picked up and immediately got a show." Another young lady who accompanied a prospective client to his audition wound up being signed by The Agency, while they passed on her scene partner.

Having agents within the company who handle producers and directors is a wonderful bonus for the actors represented by The Agency. They can network within the ranks, and if a producer is tapped for a particular project, the other agents will check out the possibilities of getting their clients involved. "It's almost like a management situation," says Gonzales. In fact, he has developed close relationships with many of his clients. "For most of them, I'm their first agent. I'm a very important part of their lives. But still, I'm an agent first. They may not like some of the advice I give them, and if I were just a friend, I don't know if I would offer that advice." They may not like it when Gonzales chastises them for conducting themselves improperly on the set or for submitting unprofessional headshots. "Sometimes clients just won't listen to my suggestions. I had a client who had great potential, but she refused to follow my advice. She never got a good role." She's obviously no longer a client of The Agency.

Not only does Gonzales criticize actors for handling themselves in an unprofessional manner, he also frowns on the way some actors fail to show the proper respect for others in the business. "This is a business of making connections," he stresses. "I see a lot of actors who have huge egos, even though they're still struggling. You have to be gracious at auditions while staying in character at the same time. It's not always easy, but those clients who understand how to do that are the clients I want." He also respects actors who continue to study their craft. "Unless you're working constantly, you have to take classes. When I get a resume, I always look at who the actor is studying with." If a client asks for suggestions, Gonzales will usually recommend Aaron Speiser or Andrew Magarian, even though they're a bit pricey. "I'll set up the appointment the first time, and occasionally I'll even go with them to audit a class." He recalls one instance when he signed an actress from Salt Lake City with little training but with a great deal of potential. "She started taking private classes and very quickly tested for a series on Showtime. She didn't get it, but she did get the next audition she went on, for the daytime show *Passions*. She admitted it had a lot to do with her coach."

Gonzales is in favor of his clients getting on stage once in a while to build credits, but with all the film and television in which he's involved, he doesn't have much time to focus on legit theater. "We do look for good material for our clients, though," he says. "If there's anything appropriate for them at the Mark Taper Forum or Lincoln Center, we'll push for it." The smaller venues are not a priority with The Agency, but building an eclectic mix of actors is. Gonzales himself is a blend of Asian and Hispanic, and he's always on the lookout for good ethnic actors. "There was an article in the trades about the lack of minority programming on television," he bemoans. "We minorities have to stick together. I'm always looking for ways of getting my clients in on projects that are not necessarily written for minorities. Sometimes it works, and sometimes it doesn't."

The best way for actors to get a break, Gonzales believes, is through networking. "This is a small town, and whoever you meet, you have to try to build on that and try to get everybody to like you." Everything, he says, happens for a reason. "If you don't get a certain job, you just have to work on the next opportunity. If it's going to happen, it's going to happen at a small agency like ours, because we're the ones who really work hard. We're not about trying to keep clients. We're about breaking people out to the level where they can choose the projects they want. That's the most satisfying part of our job."

Patty Grana-Miller

BOBBY BALL AGENCY
4342 Lankershim Boulevard
Universal City, CA 91602
(818) 506-8188
FAX (818) 506-8588

If Patty Grana-Miller is the president of the Bobby Ball Agency, who's Bobby Ball? Ask many of her clients, and they have no idea. But ask Grana-Miller, and she'll proudly tell you that it's her mom, who started the agency in Scottsdale, Arizona, more than thirty years ago. Fifteen years ago they expanded to Los Angeles. "I grew up in the business," Grana-Miller explains. She acted and modeled when she was young. In college she decided to major in cultural anthropology, and when she went on for a master's degree, she focused on international management. "That's what I really thought I wanted to do with my life, but being a twenty-one-year-old female just out of school, no one took me seriously as a contender for a government job in a Third World country." So it was back to the agency to pay for her education, and much to her surprise, she began to like it. "I seem to have a business aptitude, and I love working with actors. I find it challenging and rewarding."

The Bobby Ball Agency eventually sold its Arizona office and maintained the commercial-theatrical agency in Los Angeles, of which Grana-Miller is in charge. She also functions as a commercial agent. Today the agency has a department for just about every specialty, including children's, print, sports, music, spokesperson, choreography and dance, and Equity. (The only specialty not covered is voice-overs.) Each department has a separate client list and is a separate entity; an actor represented in print, for example, won't automatically be submitted for theatrical or commercial projects. Grana-Miller is open to representing someone in the dance department, but if the person can't handle copy well and doesn't spark her interest, it's not likely she'll take the person on as a commercial client.

Actors who are auditioning for the commercial department are asked to select two different pieces of copy, take a few minutes to look them over, and then come in and read. "It's important to see if they choose material that's suitable and to see how they handle the copy. If they read well and have a marketable look, I'm interested." Another important factor is personality. "We have to click. Does this actor fit with our image and vice versa? If it all comes together, and we have space for the actor on our client list, we'll sign him or her."

Grana-Miller loves the hectic pace of her department. "It's brutally fast," she admits. "We see the fruits of our labor very quickly. The pace is even more frantic than in the past, since time frames have gotten much shorter in the last few years.

There's not as much prep time for commercials, and the numbers have increased. So many actors do commercials in Los Angeles that the weeding-out process for the casting director is much harder. There are still a few casting directors who'll call an agent on the phone and ask for recommendations, but it's not common. Today it's picture submissions. Pitching actors is more challenging now. If a casting director calls us today with a breakdown, it's likely there's going to be an audition session tomorrow. There's little time for chit-chat."

The best way for an actor to compete in this hectic world, says Grana-Miller, is to develop good working relationships with casting directors. Make a good impression at the audition—they remember. But the process can also seem very whimsical; an actor may have been selected or eliminated for apparently arbitrary reasons. Grana-Miller offers a case in point: "One of our clients had auditioned for a commercial but didn't get a callback, but the actor she worked off at the audition was called back. He wasn't available, however, so at the callback session they reviewed him from the original videotape. Well, guess what? The producers fell in love with my client and they wound up booking her!" It was her first commercial, and both she and Grana-Miller were thrilled with the outcome. That's one of the stories with a happy ending. There are those with not-so-happy endings, too. "Another client, a comedienne we represent, had booked a national spot. She was ready to work. She went to wardrobe two days before the shoot. I get a call from the casting director. She's canceled. Why? One of the ad agency people didn't like her looks, because she reminded him of an ex-wife! How devastating. But it's out of your hands. All you can do is do the best job possible. Everything else is beyond your control."

If an actor isn't booking very much, Grana-Miller will try to find out if there's something the actor can do to improve his or her situation. "We're in it for the long haul," she states. "If there's a problem, I'll talk to the actor to see if he or she needs some time off. If it's the pictures, we'll talk about that. Maybe the actor has to tweak his or her image. One of my clients, who was very marketable, had to do some fine-tuning to get attention. She just couldn't get arrested until one day she gave herself a more '90s look, let her personality emerge, and she's working constantly now. This year she booked fifteen national commercials." Grana-Miller believes it's the nature of the business. You have to keep up with the trends and realize that there are cycles when you're hot and when you're not. "The industry is challenging," she admits. "But you must have your skills down and have a solid financial base from which to springboard and be able to take the time you need to establish yourself. Don't give yourself unrealistic limits. If you're a good actor, sooner or later it's going to happen."

Neal Hamil

FORD AGENCY
142 Greene Street
New York, NY 10012
(212) 219-6170
FAX (212) 966-1531

What better prior experience for a modeling agent than modeling? Neal Hamil worked his way through college as a model, then transitioned to the agency side in 1981. He and his sister went into partnership in Texas in 1983, running their own agency for ten years. When he sold the business in 1993, he was invited to join the prestigious Ford Agency in New York as executive vice president in charge of the women's division. His clients include Jerry Hall and Naomi Campbell, the agency's top names. He says it's a twelve-hour-a-day job.

The agency has several divisions: showroom models, classic women (thirty-five years and older), print, character faces, larger women (size twelve and up), runway, television (in conjunction with Innovative Artists), and children. "We also have a Supermodel of the World department that runs our annual contest where we select models from at least forty countries competing for a $200,000 modeling contract." The contest has been around since the late '70s. The only problem he sees with finding top models at such a young age is that many aren't ready to work. They're still in school, and the agency refuses to take anyone out of school until they've graduated.

Unlike agencies that handle only actors, Ford is always looking for potential models. Everyone is invited to submit a headshot. "It's so easy to get yourself seen by Ford," he admits. "We have offices in Chicago, Miami, Cleveland, Toronto, Los Angeles, and New York. All you have to do is take a picture with a disposable camera that shows you full length from the front, and then a couple of headshots—one from the front and a profile shot—and mail them in with your name, height, weight, measurements, and contact information." Of the two million who submit every year, Ford responds to every one. "If we're interested, we'll bring you to New York or contact one of our local affiliates. We can tell from a simple Polaroid if we're interested. But even if we're not, we'll let you know."

Of course, if you're gorgeous, there's always a place for you in the fashion industry; yet there are also opportunities for those who are not. They may not be runway or cover models, but with commercial print work, the range is much greater. "The trends are always changing," says Hamil. "A few years ago shapeless was in, and today it seems the classic shape is coming back. They're looking for sexy, beautiful girls. It's a lot more exciting to sell someone who's truly beautiful."

The other day a girl came in with a couple of pictures. They signed her on the spot. She's a knockout, but two years ago they wouldn't have even considered her because of her figure. You have to always keep in mind what's 'in.'" It's much the same story for male models. Hamil suggests picking up a few fashion magazines to get an idea of today's look.

Hamil believes that modeling is a great training ground for actors. More models, he says, are going into film after a successful career in print or commercials. "We see more scripts being sent to our clients all the time. Some of our success stories include Kelly LeBrock, Catherine Oxenberg, and Cheryl Tiegs. They were the leaders. Today, it's models like Naomi Campbell and Tomiko Fraser. They're naturals." Men, he says, usually don't see modeling as a career. They're often recruited rather than actively seeking placement. "A lot of male models get discovered. The first person I found was at the Broadway Diner in New Jersey on New Year's Eve. I approached him, and he came aboard. Now he's in the Marine Corps." Ford represents about ninety males and is always on the lookout for men. "For males, you need lots of personality. You have to be between six feet and six feet two inches and wear a forty long. The ideal age is between eighteen and twenty-four for high fashion. For catalogue work it extends to twenty-six." Hamil says that 60 percent of male models try to break into film and television, but only about 5 percent make it. Some of the successful transitions include Billy Baldwin, Matthew Fox, and Scott Wolf.

Andrea Wilner heads up the kids' division, which handles children from three months to nineteen years. Their clients run the gamut from print to television work. Wilner says that Ford is definitely seeking an ethnic mix, and she looks at every picture that comes across her desk. The one requirement is that the kids must be outgoing, quick to warm up, and comfortable with a lot of people. The more vivacious a child is, the more that child will work. Wilner suggests sending a simple snapshot to be considered for representation, since the agency doesn't want families to invest a lot of money in photographs unless they have to. Once children are signed, they'll need professional pictures for a composite. The most popular catalogue sizes for kids are three, five, and ten for girls; three, five, and twelve for boys. It's a lot tougher, says Wilner, to find boys willing to model once they enter junior high school and get actively involved in sports. If they're willing to put their energy into modeling, she offers, there's a lot of work available.

Do you need to go to modeling school to be a model? Definitely not, says Hamil. If you get a call from a modeling school asking you to apply, suggesting it's the way into the business, beware. "Modeling schools are the finishing schools of this generation," says Hamil, "particularly in the South. They do very well, because families are keen on polishing their daughters. But you don't need to go to school to be a model. I'm sure most of the top models never set foot in one." If you have the right ingredients and are willing to work hard, just submit your snapshots to a reputable agency and you may get a phone call. Just be sure it's not a scam. If they ask for money before you're earning it, continue your search.

Kathy Hardegree

ATLANTA MODELS
AND TALENT, INC.
2970 Peachtree Road NW, #600
Atlanta, GA 30305
(404) 261-9627
FAX (404) 231-5410

Forty years ago, Kathy Hardegree wouldn't have dreamed she'd be the owner of one of Atlanta's most successful talent agencies. She had just been laid off from her secretarial position, and job opportunities for young women in Atlanta were scarce. Her hairstylist happened to mention that one of her clients who owned a talent agency needed someone to decorate a couple of wig shops she was opening. Desperate to earn some money, she was disappointed when the wig shop owner confessed that all their money was tied up in the shops, and they could only afford to pay Hardegree one hundred dollars a week. Having nowhere to turn, she took the job with the promise that they would find a place for her down the line in their organization. "I started answering the phones at the agency, and after three months I volunteered to alphabetize the clients' pictures, since they were piled up everywhere. They loved that idea. They made me feel I'd just invented sliced bread!" A year later, Hardegree was president of the corporation, and four years after that, she owned the company.

Atlanta is not the biggest city for theatrical opportunities, but it can be rewarding for actors. There are times when there's lots of work. "*In the Heat of the Night* shot here for seven years," Hardegree notes. "They employed an enormous number of actors for both principal and recurring roles. The Film and Video Commission works very hard to sell Georgia, which has one of the very first film commissions outside Los Angeles and New York. In 1973, then-governor Jimmy Carter signed a bill establishing the commission." They have a steady supply of nonunion commercials and union industrials. "We're also working a lot on the Internet when they need someone's voice or image, and there's also quite a bit of print and voice-over work."

Atlanta Models and Talent is a full-service agency for commercial, theatrical, voice-over, and print, with a client roster ranging from age six to senior citizen. The agency represents close to 300 actors, but only about 100 work consistently. "We are looking for actors who are quick sells," explains Hardegree, "those who've studied their craft so that they can create magic when they go on an audition or get hired." She looks at every headshot that passes her desk as well as hundreds of videotapes a year, and signs only about three or four new clients a month. Most of the clients come from submissions, although some are referrals. "If we're interested in an actor, we want to see tape. If they don't have a tape, we suggest they put a monologue on a camcorder and bring it to us. I want to see what they can do in front of a camera with no one else in the room."

If an actor has promise but not much experience, Hardegree will refer him or her to one of a dozen acting classes in the city. "We don't have master classes like in New York or Los Angeles," she admits, "but there are a number of good schools, especially for those just getting started." Once the actor has graduated, Hardegree suggests work in community theater, eventually working up to Equity productions. "Usually at that point, once they've built their acting craft, they can take on-camera technique classes and find an agent." Among those who built their craft in Atlanta prior to moving to Los Angeles are Dennis Haskins of *Saved by the Bell* and veteran film star Samuel L. Jackson. "Joe Dorothy moved here from New York and later joined the cast of *Murder She Wrote*." And then there's Vanna White's story. "I kept pushing her to take acting classes while she was modeling here in Atlanta," Hardegree recalls. "But she just wanted to model. Next thing I knew she was on *Wheel of Fortune*."

Hardegree is fortunate to have been in Atlanta for as many years as she has. Some of those who've become casting directors are former clients or employees. "I have very good relationships with most casting directors in town, and if someone new pops up, I make it my business to get to know them." The only breakdowns to which Hardegree subscribes are those in Atlanta. If there's a national casting search going on, however, she'll definitely get involved. But she won't get involved with agent workshops. "I just don't want to take money from actors. I'll talk to students, though, at various drama schools and speak at modeling conventions."

Hardegree tells Hollywood hopefuls to keep their headshots and resumes up to date and videos current. "You can't have a demo with brown hair if you're now a blond," she insists. One of the most frequently asked questions at her lectures is: How do you know you should become an actor? "I tell them to train and work very hard for five or ten years and see what kind of success you have. If it's more than just your family and friends patting you on the back, perhaps you're good at it and should continue to pursue it." Another common question: What are you supposed to do at an audition? "Make magic! Make those words come off the page, because if you can do that, whether you're auditioning for a commercial or film, there's a good chance you're going to win."

Paul Hilepo

MICHAEL HARTIG
AGENCY, LTD.
156 Fifth Avenue, #820
New York, NY 10010
(212) 252-9670
FAX (212) 929-1266

The Michael Hartig Agency in New York is considered a boutique agency. It consists of three agents who represent about seventy-five actors for theater, film, and television. Paul Hilepo has been with the agency since he first started in this business six years ago, making his way up from assistant to full-fledged agent in just two years. "You learn the guidelines you have to work under, develop your communications skills, and acquire the rapport you need to get good clients," Hilepo explains. "I certainly didn't learn how to be an agent in college! There are no courses in school that teach you this business. You just have to get in there and learn."

Having a small agency keeps the competition within less frenetic. "It's hard enough for actors to be competing with every other actor from every other agency in New York, so we try not to have conflicts within the office." They do this by maintaining an eclectic group of actors ranging from those fresh out of school to those who've garnered the coveted Oscar. Clients include Jerry Stiller (*Seinfeld, King of Queens*), Tyne Daly (*Cagney & Lacey, Judging Amy*), Earl Hindman (*Home Improvement,*) and film star Mercedes McCambridge. The agency also represents up-and-coming actors and talented fledglings who aren't even in the union. "I think union status is very overrated," Hilepo declares. "In fact, I tend to tell my actors not to rush to join any union, because they could get lots of work in projects like student films and nonequity theater. They can really build up their resumes and reels, and when someone decides to hire that actor, all they'll have to do is sign some paperwork and come up with union dues."

Most clients come from referrals and submissions. "I go through all my mail," Hilepo insists. "I've found superb actors through direct mailings." He also attends showcases and end-of-the-year productions presented by the fine university drama schools. And then there are the occasions when Hilepo will walk down the street or into a restaurant and ask someone interesting, "Are you an actor?" "It happens," he admits. "In fact, I remember being at a birthday party and seeing an attractive young man tending bar. I was with an agent friend of mine, and we started chatting, and it turned out the bartender was indeed an actor. You never know where you're going to make connections." That's why Hilepo suggests that actors showcase and do as much theater as they can, to expose themselves to as many agents and casting people as possible. "I generally go to the theater at least twice a week," says Hilepo. "If I know a good actor is in a production, I assume the others in the cast will be pretty good. I try to go to almost every show my clients are doing here in New York just to lend support. I'm the one who tells them to get involved with theater, so I feel it's my responsibility to be there."

He also believes that actors are better served by keeping busy doing something related to the business and their craft, not just waiting tables and waiting for the big break. "I feel their psyches are so fragile anyway that if they're making money in the business, even if it's not TV or film, they'll be happier than doing a 'civilian' job. It helps keep their spirits up. And as an active participant, I really believe when they do get a chance to audition for that film, they'll go in there knowing they belong there, because they've been keeping busy honing their skills." Hilepo has seen careers blossom from one small appearance in a showcase. "Once, when my boss had to find something to do when his weekend plans were suddenly canceled, he went to a little showcase down in the East Village. He spotted an actress in the show who was seeking representation and called her in. She was really good. We started working with her; within twenty-four hours he got her a national tour at $3,000 a week and she's currently earning a quarter of a million dollars a year."

Hilepo is a strong advocate of theater. "It all goes back to that old saying, 'You can't fake it on stage.' There are no cuts, no double takes, no between-scene directions. But securing a theater job in New York is not easy." Hilepo goes through the daily breakdowns to see which shows are being cast. Often project information will be disseminated directly through casting directors. Open calls are listed in the trade journals. "It involves getting up very early in the morning and waiting in line possibly the entire day until you're auditioned, and an actor's odds are not that great. But I've seen clients get callbacks at open calls; and again, you never know whom you'll meet." The difference between theater and on-camera auditions, he explains, is that theater usually offers more time for the actor to prepare. "On-camera auditions usually provide a day's notice, whereas with theater, you may have a week to prepare. That allows the actor time to really study the material." As with film and television, there's also a callback process, and it can be lengthy, especially for Broadway shows.

Hilepo warns that without a strong resume and solid training, it's nearly impossible to get into a Broadway show, although exceptions do happen. "The odds don't keep me from being persistent. I've broken down doors and had actors seen regardless of their credits. I've had actors book major jobs from my insisting the casting director see my clients. Just like anything in life, if you really believe in what you're saying and who you're saying it for, you can't describe the strength. It's nothing you can put into words."

What he can put into words, however, is his love of the industry. "I adore theater, film, and television. I also have a high respect for actors. I learn so much from them, but one thing they should learn is to take it one step at a time. Actors must stop writing their Oscar acceptance speeches the second they enter the business. Planning way ahead is dangerous; you should focus on life on a day-to-day basis and see where it takes you. You really have to surrender control in this business, because it's an ever-changing market. It's better to focus on perfecting your craft. Actors need to take responsibility for their careers. I really feel that hard work, conviction, and belief in what one is doing is admired and respected, and industry professionals tend to notice that." Hilepo says he can't see himself doing anything else in his life, and he admires actors who feel likewise. "I gravitate toward those who are hard-working, talented, and motivated. That's the secret a lot of people don't understand, and that's really what it's all about."

Jerry Hogan

HENDERSON/HOGAN
850 Seventh Avenue, #1003
New York, NY 10019
(212) 765-5190
FAX (212) 586-2855

What does an actor do when acting doesn't seem to be leading to financial independence? Well, for Jerry Hogan, agenting seemed the most logical choice. Hogan spent several years in musical theater—first in Kentucky, then Texas, and ultimately New York. To help pay the bills while pounding the pavement, he started working as a secretary for a successful talent agent in New York, who encouraged Hogan to pursue the business as an agent since he seemed to have a flair for the field. "I liked it," he admits. "I felt that it was fun and a lot more secure than being an actor." After working for Margaret Henderson they eventually established a partnership, which has blossomed into a bicoastal agency representing some 300 clients.

While actors can be represented on both coasts, Hogan doesn't guarantee that every client will have that opportunity. "People need to have chemistry and know each other before committing to a relationship. If an agent in Los Angeles doesn't know the client in New York, why would he put a lot of effort into finding the person work when he has other actors in L.A. to whom he's committed?" The two offices do work together, however, and if they know an actor is moving to the opposite coast, they'll try to accommodate.

Hogan is looking for actors who are intelligent and trained. "Sometimes just a 'look' will give me the incentive to call an actor. Then, when we meet, it has to be followed up by diligence and a determination to work hard." He recalls meeting an actor who was introduced to him by a relative. "He didn't have any experience but had a tremendous personality and drive. He looked at this as a business. He made sure he had his pictures and resumes up to date, took a variety of classes, did showcases and theater. He didn't just hang around waiting for me to call." Hogan saw something special in this actor, who's now out in Hollywood doing lead roles in film and television. "It's not easy selling an actor with little experience," Hogan admits, "but if you tell casting directors that this actor is incredible, and this extremely above-average person walks into the audition and performs, they'll remember, and it makes it easier the next time."

The agency has found clients through referrals, submissions, and reputable theater schools. "I have a client now," Hogan recalls, "whom we saw at a graduation showcase put on by his school. He was wonderful. He went on to the Berkshires the following summer, and I invited a casting director to see him perform." That led to his being auditioned for a one-man show in Washington, D.C., where he got great reviews and was nominated for a Helen Hayes award. "He's currently on Broadway in *Epic Proportions,* because of his determination and hard work as well as his fine talent."

If Hogan isn't familiar with an actor's work, he'll have him or her prepare a monologue or scene for the agents in the office. He's not as focused on the actor's resume as he is on the actor as a person. "An actor with charisma can make any role or experience come to life and catch my attention, no matter how insignificant it may appear on a resume. I just want them to be able to keep the conversation going. That's what we're looking for in our clients. They have to be able to communicate, because they're the ones performing. We need to see they're alive and sure of themselves." What he's not looking for is the actor who's doing this for the wrong reason. "One guy came in and said he had decided he wanted to act. When I asked him why, he said, 'Beats working!' I said, Thank you very much, nice meeting you."

Most of the actors with whom Henderson/Hogan work are affiliated with the unions, but that doesn't mean the agency won't take someone on who's just getting into the field. "If actors are young and recently out of school, I'd simply work with them until they got a job, so they could be Taft-Harley-ed into the union." But loyalty isn't a one-way street. Hogan insists on exclusivity with his actors. All must sign with the agency to be represented. "I have people who've been with us for twenty-six years," he says. "It's usually the actors who bail out, not us. Once they get successful they feel they need a bigger name to represent them. It's unfortunate, but that's the nature of the business."

Henderson/Hogan represents actors of all ages and types. Several of their better-known clients have been around for decades, such as Ann Francis and Edward Albert, but Hogan admits young is in. An actor in his or her early twenties should find it relatively easy to get an appointment with an agent. "Of course, if an actor is primarily interested in theater, it's a different story. It's a lot more flexible. But the networks want young faces now, which makes it very tough for anyone over thirty. That doesn't mean you aren't good. You just don't have as much opportunity." He does admit the business is cyclical, and even though young is in today, that may change next season. "Acting is a business, not a game. You have to commit to it. You have to trust your agent. If you don't, you shouldn't be with him or her. Give yourself time, because it takes time to succeed. Continuity is the best thing in an actor's life."

John Hugh

THE ANN WAUGH AGENCY
4741 Laurel Canyon Boulevard, #200
North Hollywood, CA 91607
(818) 980-0141
FAX (818) 980-4835

Step into John Hugh's office in North Hollywood and you'll find a tall, attractive woman sitting in a chair facing the door, wearing dark glasses, with legs crossed and one shoe casually dangling from her foot. Is this one of Hugh's clients or a friend who has stopped by for a chat? And why is she staring at you? Then, much to your surprise, you realize that it's only a mannequin. A mannequin?! "One year, my wife asked me what I wanted for my birthday. I said, 'I don't need anything, but I've always wanted a mannequin.' A few days later, sitting at the dining room table was a mannequin dressed in one of my suits. That afternoon UPS delivered another one, a female, and we named them Bo and Derek." Hugh left Derek at home, while Bo graces his office, keeping him company. "When people ask me who this mannequin is, I say she's a friend who died, and we had her stuffed."

That's John Hugh, an iconoclast. He has been an agent for ten years, following a less-than-brilliant career as an actor. "Ann Waugh had been my agent, and when I found out she was retiring to Oregon and was selling the business, I asked if I could take it over." Done deal. Does he miss the life of the actor? "When you're an actor and don't get the job, you think, 'Oh, what did I do? I could have, should have. . . .' I don't miss those feelings one bit. As an agent, you think, 'We didn't get that one. Maybe we'll get the next one.' When you get a callback, I get nearly as excited as you. We're both very happy. That's what I enjoy."

Hugh distinguishes himself as an agent by being what he calls "the tallest Chinaman in this town." He stands six feet one. His clients call him their "Asiant," as in Asian agent, since he's a blend of Chinese and Irish. "I'm also very honest with my clients," he admits. "I let actors know that first and foremost this is a business, not just a look or an opportunity to display your talent. There are hundreds of talented people in this town who don't work. It's sad. You have to know how to market yourself as an actor."

Hugh finds his clients mostly through referrals from casting directors and other actors. Occasionally a photo and resume will come across his desk that interests him, and he'll bring the actor in and sign him or her. "You obviously go by the picture," he explains. "I'll call them in if they have an unusual or quirky look. We like unusual looks more than Hollywood beauties at this agency. I'll talk to them, get to know them a little. See if they can read and how well. Make sure they're in class and keeping up with their craft." He's especially critical of the actor who steps off the bus from a small town expecting to hit it big in Hollywood merely because she's a local beauty queen. "They think this is the Valley of the Dolls, and it's not. It's a profession at which you have to work hard, study, and fine-tune your instrument." Of course, if you're eighteen and can play younger, you do have an advantage over a thirty-year-old, who is much harder to cast. Casting directors, however, often turn to Hugh when they're seeking the more unusual character. "I know a lot of Asian actors from having been an Asian actor for many years, but I represent character actors of all persuasions. If we're known for anything it might be character minorities."

If a breakdown calls for a specific character to be portrayed by a Caucasian, Hugh will try to persuade the casting director to go in a different direction if it's appropriate. "There's a project pending right now where they're looking for television-host types, which traditionally means beautiful men and women. I called and suggested someone who's anything but beautiful. He's short and pudgy, and he's a minority. He got a callback. He even got a second callback, and the casting director admitted he was amazed at the response. He told me the actor came in and tap-danced his way around the producers and other actors, and so far he's at the top in the running."

Not all agents take risks, but Hugh is one who seems unafraid. He won't, however, pester casting directors, asking for feedback after every audition. "They just don't have the time, and when actors ask if I've gotten feedback, I tell them to focus instead on doing the best job they can—then go home and do their gardening. I remember a casting director told me once that an agent had called him for some feedback, which was very negative. A couple of weeks later the casting director was waiting in front of a movie theater in Hollywood when the actor walked up and confronted him with 'So you don't think I'm any good, huh?' A lot of crazy people are out there."

Fortunately, there are a lot of wonderful people as well. One of Hugh's favorites is an older woman who had been his neighbor for seven years while he was still an actor. When he finally bought the agency he called her up and invited her over to see the place. "She brought me a basket of cheeses and wine to congratulate me. She told me she had just retired as a music secretary. The agency was looking for a little old lady type, so we took some pictures of her. They were terrible, but they captured her eccentric qualities, and she started booking. By her third audition she was hired. She made so much money the first year, she was taken off social security." Of course not all stories have such happy endings, but quick success or not, Hugh expects his actors to be confident. "You've got to be able to go to an audition and kick major butt. Come out saying you did a good job. One of my actors who always gets a callback once told me that whenever he reads for a new casting director he knows he's not necessarily auditioning for the role he's called in for. He's auditioning for maybe the fifth job down the road. He says, 'I do a good job so they remember me and call me back.' It works. You better be good, because if you're bad, they're certainly going to remember that!"

Marcia Hurwitz

SPECIAL ARTISTS AGENCY, INC.
Partner: Liz Dalling
Agents: Joy Kelly, celebrities; Laura Fogelman, on-camera;
Mark Measures, on-camera; Jenine Leigh, on-camera;
Kelly Gursey, models; Luanne Salandy, voice-over

345 North Maple Drive, #3020
Beverly Hills, CA 90210
(310) 859-9688
FAX (310) 859-9020

When you enter the Beverly Hills office of Marcia Hurwitz, you get the feeling this woman is not a "corporate" type. This is no Los Angeles high-rise with sterile cubicles and black leather chairs. Hurwitz conducts her business surrounded by natural wood furnishings, photos of family and friends, and leafy maple trees peeking into her third-story window. A transplant from New York, where she began as an agent twenty-four years ago, Hurwitz has been in Los Angeles for the last twenty-one years. To what does she attribute her interest in agenting? "It was being in the right place at the right time," she reveals. "Someone came up to me and said, 'I think you'd be very good at this. Would you like to give it a try?'" And that's pretty much the way it fell into place. "I was doing special events at a New York department store. I had just finished conducting a workshop for teens with someone who ran a modeling agency. She remembered me when she lost one of her head bookers and offered me the job." It was the '70s, the peak of the fashion business in New York. "I loved it. Since I wanted to grow, I moved into the television department and became an agent. Bill Cunningham [a top agent in Los Angeles] brought me out to California to join his agency in 1977. He was my mentor." She worked for Cunningham for three years, then left to found Special Artists with her friend Liz Dalling.

Special Artists has three on-camera agents, and Hurwitz runs the voice-over department. As a commercial agency, it's deluged with submissions and needs a large support staff. "Running a commercial agency is a little more satisfying than theatrical," Hurwitz believes, "because you get the bookings a lot sooner." The bookings for each client, she explains, come from all the agents, who work as a team. "That's because we have to know every one of these people, and they have to know us, since we're submitting huge numbers of people every day. We divide up the casting directors among our agents so that each casting director knows the particular agent he or she is dealing with, and can always call upon the strength of that agent at any time."

Hurwitz likens her agency to a boutique, despite its 650 clients. "It's not so much the numbers," she says. "It's the way we run the agency. We don't take on the masses. We only work with actors we sign, unlike in New York, where agents often handle freelancers as well. You can't nurture a career if you don't have a hands-on relationship with each client. That's our philosophy, and it helps get our clients through the hard times, so that when the good times come along everyone can reap the benefits." Clients are filtered into Special Artists from casting directors, East Coast agencies, word of mouth, and theatrical agents. "It's vital to keep up relationships with theatrical agents," stresses Hurwitz. "If we get their client one job, and the client does it well, we'll likely get another client, and a relationship forms. We don't always share clients with a specific agency, but we'll always consider them."

Without a recommendation, it's very difficult to get through the door at Special Artists. "We'll always look through any submissions we get, but you'd need an incredible resume with a great theatrical background for us to consider representing you." If such a submission does cross her desk, she says, and she's in a situation where they don't have someone in that category, she may call the actor in for an interview. Hurwitz is careful about conflicts. Due to the relatively small number of actors she represents, she feels it's critical not to have too many in one category. "You know when the casting director calls, and you get all ten of your actors in for the reading, you're doing your job. No one gets sacrificed. You're representing each and every actor."

Once an actor does get a foot in the door, he or she has to meet all the on-camera agents. "And honestly," Hurwitz divulges, "it's the personality as well as the photo and resume that are important. We don't have a crystal ball. If we haven't seen an actor's work, we really don't know. It's a gut feeling that comes from experience and sizing up all the information." First impressions are very important to Hurwitz. "The way you look represents the way you live, and the way you look when you go out on interviews reflects on us. We need to know that you won't embarrass us." Another important attribute is an actor's attitude. "If you try to give an actor tips and the person argues with you, you're not on the same wavelength. An actor should be able to take constructive criticism."

Hurwitz is wary of actors who speak negatively about others in the business. "It turns us all off," she declares. "We feel if they do it about someone else, they could do it about us." What impresses the agents are actors who ask intelligent questions. "If actors ask us for feedback on their tapes or pictures, we know the person is open to suggestions. If they think they know it all, then why do they need us?"

The workload in the voice-over department consists of animation, feature films, CD-ROMS, trailers, and promos. In order to get an interview with Hurwitz in this department, you usually need a voice-over tape. "If I see their videotape and see they're really talented, however, I can sense the voice-over situation, and I'll bring them in. It's more an actor's department than a strictly voice-over department," explains Hurwitz, who never allows actors to put together reels on their own. "If they need a tape, I work very closely with the actor and producer. They can't possibly know what I want. They don't know how we like to market them." Hurwitz needs to get an idea of what the actor's strengths are, what kind of personality he or she has, and how the agents will be able to promote the client in the marketplace.

A voice-over actor may be running around all day on auditions, Hurwitz cautions. "It's a highly competitive field, fast and furious. It's popular because you can make more money in a day than an on-camera actor and get more jobs that are not dependent solely on this market." Most of the voice-over work is still dominated by males, she confesses.

Special Artists has two voice-over booths, which accommodate the large amount of audition material that comes along. "The bad news," Hurwitz admits, "is that it costs a lot of money, and we need to do a huge volume of business to make it worthwhile." Assistants direct the casting sessions, but if a client needs guidance, Hurwitz will be there in the booth. Her client list includes about 120 voice-over actors, who are instructed to keep their beepers functioning at all times and their energy at maximum capacity.

Special Artists doesn't have a children's department per se, but for those clients who have kids, Hurwitz says she'll consider representing them if they're qualified and talented. "We've booked lots of children on-camera and for voice-overs, but we try to keep it in the family." Print is another area not normally covered by Special Artists, but Kelly Gursey, one of the agents, works closely with Elite Models, representing many of their clients.

"We had a vision when we started," Hurwitz imparts. "We wouldn't be fast food. We'd be proactive. We'd see where we could further a career, foreseeing changes in the business and going along with them. We can't promise anything, only to do our best to care and be human. We make sure our clients know we're behind them." If an actor hasn't worked in two years and doesn't make big bucks, Hurwitz doesn't automatically cut him or her from the list. "We all go through good times and bad times," she says. "Actors will part company with us sooner than we'll part company with them. The only time we'll release them is if they're not treating someone here with respect." To Hurwitz, the most critical issue is understanding. "I think that makes a big difference in their lives, and I think it's vital for them to know that their agent cares."

Craig Jones

FILM/THEATRE
ACTORS' EXCHANGE
582 Market Street, #306
San Francisco, CA 94104
(415) 433-3920
FAX (415) 433-3922

A self-proclaimed frustrated-actor-turned-agent, Craig Jones started out teaching acting at a public high school in San Francisco after realizing that his own acting career didn't seem to be going anywhere. He decided to become an agent after establishing a film and theater actors' exchange, a referral service for student filmmakers and actors. "It was a successful venture, finding actors who were willing to volunteer for student film projects. There was no other local place where directors could turn. I was driving around North Beach and happened to see a 'For Rent' sign above the City Lights Bookstore. That was my first office, where I began placing my actor friends." Jones charged both actors and filmmakers five dollars a year. "If I got twenty people a month to join, I had my rent covered. Those who helped out in the office were volunteers. Two hundred student films later, I found myself casting industrials and becoming an agent." He got his official license in 1980.

Still called the Film/Theatre Actors' Exchange, Jones handles about fifty actors primarily for commercials and industrials, although he occasionally places actors in print and voice-over jobs. "I have a high regard for theater-trained actors," he admits, "but theater doesn't usually pay the bills, so I try to get my clients films and commercials so they can afford to pursue their art." The serious actors in town work at Berkeley Rep, American Conservatory Theater (ACT), the San Jose Stage Company, and San Jose Rep. "If they've only done theater, I encourage them to take commercial and film classes so they can better make that transition." For nonunion actors, Jones is confident that by the time they get that first job, they'll be ready to join. "I must say, however, that while there's quite a bit of extra work in film up here, there isn't much work for principals. About the only union show they're shooting here right now is *Nash Bridges.*" According to Jones, San Francisco has about nine or ten agents, and most make their living from commercials. He himself has placed actors in Wrigley's, Pillsbury, Citibank, and First Union Bank spots.

Most of those interested in representation send in a photo and resume, and an invitation to see them on stage. "I don't like auditioning actors in the office. I much prefer seeing them working with other actors, because that way I can better judge how well they listen and interact." In an office situation, he says, actors seem to focus on the agent, which he finds distracting. If he's sufficiently impressed with the quality of an actor's stage performance, he'll then invite the actor to his office to chat. "That's when I decide whether we can work together. If the actor's ego is larger than his or her talent, I certainly won't be interested. Actors should be able to place themselves realistically in the marketplace. I should be telling them how great they are, not vice versa." Attitude is important, both on and off the set. "I remember when one of my actors was cast in a film about prisoners on Alcatraz. When the director asked him to do the scene a different way, he told the director, 'I don't tell you how to direct. Don't tell me how to act!' He was lucky he didn't get fired, but it's definitely not the way to endear yourself to those in the position to hire you in the future."

Jones doesn't want his clients competing with one another, so he prefers handling only a few people who fit in a similar category, rather than ten of the same type. "But it makes it difficult for me. If an actor doesn't show up for an audition, I'm out of luck. I haven't submitted several actors for the role, so if my one or two aren't in the running, I don't get a commission." Jones also works without contracts. "The business is slow enough," he submits. "I figure since it's so easy to get out of a contract, why bother? If someone wants to work with me, and it's mutual, it's a much more comfortable situation." Not only do actors feel comfortable working with Jones, ditto for most casting directors in town. He has been in the area for so many years, everyone knows and respects him.

There are agent showcases in San Francisco, but Jones isn't interested in participating. "I don't think actors should have to pay agents and casting directors to see them perform. I just don't feel it's right." He'd rather do the paying, and he does, attending lots of theater in a city known for its fine productions. But fine acting isn't the only thing on which Jones focuses. He's always explaining to actors that this is a business that requires years of training and experience. "Your head has to be screwed on straight. You have to have a realistic approach and expectations. Should you get lucky and become famous, that's gravy. But my advice: Just become a working actor."

Doug Kesten

PARADIGM, A TALENT
& LITERARY AGENCY
200 West 57th Street, #900
New York, NY 10019
(212) 246-1030
FAX (212) 246-1521

It was difficult for Doug Kesten to avoid show business. It was in the blood. His father was an accountant for Jujamcyn, which owned and managed legitimate theaters in New York and Boston, among other cities. "I was going to shows when I was a little kid, and I had friends on Broadway. I guess I've always had a passion for theater." Being an agent was not his goal, but once he got his feet wet, he took to it as the proverbial duck to water. "The exposure to theater all those years gave me a step up. I was familiar with a lot of performers and what they were capable of and how versatile they might be. It was something I didn't have to learn."

So why did Kesten become a commercial agent if his interests were in the theater? "It just sort of happened," he shrugs. "I worked at Celebrity Service, an information and research bureau that *Good Morning America* might contact if it wanted to book a celebrity. After working the phones summers and part-time during my undergraduate junior and senior years at Columbia [University], I became the editor of *Celebrity Bulletin,* [Celebrity Service's] daily publication. It was great, but I knew if I stayed too long I'd never leave. I realized that where I belonged was in a position to find and develop talent. I was offered a job at Jacobson-Wilder, and even though they only represented actors for commercials, many of their clients were active in soap operas, film, and on Broadway. I knew I'd be exposed to some of that as well, so I took the job." That was 1979. Eventually he became a partner in the firm, which was sold to SEM&M in 1990. He stayed on for four years, at which time he moved on to Paradigm.

Kesten feels that his strength is discovering talent. "The thing that really makes me tick is finding talented individuals who are not yet in the union and putting my energy behind them." That's not to say that Paradigm takes on a lot of new-comers. "We really are selective," he points out. "Our signed client list is fairly small, just a couple of hundred actors." That may seem like a lot, but when there are five agents working full-time, Kesten believes, clients are not getting short changed. Yet that's not to say Paradigm doesn't look outside its rosters for talent. Unlike the scene in Los Angeles, many New York agents will find work for free-lance actors who are not signed with them. "The business has changed over the years to the extent that there are only two agencies in New York today that claim to work only with signed clients, Don Buchwald and CED." In Kesten's opinion, it's not realistic to think you can satisfy everyone with a limited number of clients. "I don't believe you're going to be valuable to casting directors or book as much as you're capable of booking by not looking outside your exclusive talent pool. The fact is, casting directors always want to meet new people. They're pressured into doing that from the get-go when they're hired to do the job. So you send in your established actors as well as some new faces, and chances are you'll be 'waving' someone into the union, and everyone's happy."

Kesten recalls the time he was casting a commercial for MasterCard. It was being directed by Jim Sheridan, who was at the helm of the small but powerful film *My Left Foot* and who rarely directs commercials. "I had just met a woman who had been an acting teacher and had done a lot of regional theater. She had never done a commercial and had recently relocated to New York. I had just placed her in my freelance file. I felt she was perfect for this particular spot. I submitted her, and she booked it!"

Paradigm often shares clients with other agencies in New York, such as the Gersh Agency, Innovative Artists, and J. Michael Bloom. Gersh doesn't have a commercial department, and Bloom may only be interested in certain actors for theatrical representation, thereby permitting their clients to be associated with Paradigm for commercial representation. In Los Angeles, however, Paradigm doesn't have a commercial department, and New York may inherit some of the theatrical clients who want to do commercials on the East Coast. And if Paradigm's New York clients are heading to California, the agency will try to hook them up with commercial agents on the West Coast. Kesten has this caveat, however: "Introductions are arranged, but no promises made as far as who's going to land where."

Casting directors call Paradigm with breakdowns for specific jobs. The agency also uses Breakdown Services, yet according to Kesten, most of the auditions come through calls to the agency. "They'll call and tell us there's a Sprint spot, for instance. They'll give us the premise, the breakdown of what they're looking for, that they'll be casting for three days next week, when the callbacks are going to be—that kind of information. Then the scheduling starts." That usually takes at least a couple of days, says Kesten. "We'll make lists, send some clients out, get feedback, go back to the table, adjust our lists, and come up with a few people that are funny or better looking, older or younger, depending on the feedback." And this goes on, he adds, with at least half a dozen agents working on meeting the needs of the ad agency. "They are definitely going to see as many people from as many sources as possible. Rarely does any of this stuff get done quickly any more."

Many successful commercial actors go out on seven or eight auditions a day if they're represented both on-camera and for voice-over, but Kesten says his clients may have a couple of weeks like that, which may be followed by a couple of weeks of sporadic appointments. "It's the roller-coaster existence of an actor," he acknowledges. "Somebody may have a blockbuster year and then have a year with absolutely no bookings. It doesn't mean I kick him or her out onto the street. It just means it's just not happening for that actor at this time. If actors have a history with you, and you believe in their talent, you have to hang in there; at least I do." Even when Kesten has a freelance actor who has mesmerized him in some theatrical venture but has been unable to provide immediate, consistent auditioning activity, he "won't throw away the card. I'll keep him or her in my file, hoping to make it happen sooner or later."

Like other union-franchised agencies, Paradigm signs a one-year contract with clients. Then when renewals come up, the agency has the option to renew for one, two, or three years, on an individual basis with each client. Sometimes a client will be signed across the board, meaning on-camera and voice-over, and sometimes not. "We wouldn't want to sign somebody who's really interested in voice-overs unless the voice-over department felt they could really focus on him or her," Kesten explains. "Some actors just aren't cut out for voice-overs, while others don't want to be seen on camera. Again, it's based on the individual."

Paradigm hasn't yet become entrenched in on-line casting. "I don't see the benefit," Kesten admits. "I think New York casting directors need a personal consultation with an agent. What if they find someone on-line only to discover that the actor is unavailable? Why waste precious time when everything's happening so quickly? If they call and ask me for a Winona Ryder type, I'll submit immediately and get them actors who are readily available and who will show up the next day."

As far as what kind of actors Kesten is seeking, it's more about talent than type, and he's good at spotting talent. That's why he has remained in the business for so long. "So flash forward. I have the reputation of being a commercial agent now, even though I adore theater, but transitioning into legit would be a big step backward for me. It's hard to build a reputation, just to give it up and prove myself over again in a different segment of the business. To this day, I wake up loving to go to work and loving what I do. You know the old saying, 'If it ain't broke, don't fix it!'"

John Kimble

WILLIAM MORRIS AGENCY
151 South El Camino Drive
Beverly Hills, CA 90212
(310) 859-4000
FAX (310) 859-4462

John Kimble represents another success story of a man who started in the mailroom and worked his way to the top. He began his career as an agent in one of the most famous mailrooms in the world: the one at the William Morris Agency in New York. "It was the only agency I'd heard of. Johnny Carson used to make jokes about it in his monologues. I figured it was the place to be." Kimble was impatient, however, and after two and a half years he was lured to another firm as a full-fledged agent, where he remained for the next five years. His ambition not yet slaked, Kimble started his own agency—one that continued to expand and merge until it became the renowned Triad Agency, which was bought out by none other than William Morris in 1992. "So I'm back where I started," he laughs. The only difference is that now he's on the West Coast.

The William Morris Agency is one of the largest in the world, with offices in New York, California, London, and Nashville and affiliates in Rome and Munich. Kimble runs the television talent department in the Beverly Hills office. "At any given time we probably have several hundred actors in our talent pool, ranging from unknowns to series regulars such as George Clooney and Jason Alexander." In fact, the William Morris Agency boasts at least 100 actors working as series regulars on television, and it's not luck. There are twelve agents in the television talent department alone. That's big. And those agents have the benefit of the company's wealth of industry information behind them. "Because we represent writers, directors, and producers, we're involved with a project from its conception," Kimble expounds. "The smaller agencies don't get involved until the script is already written and rewritten and has been given the green light by the producer. Here, our clients get the first shot and often set the prototype for the lead characters. They become the characters to beat. As you go along, you always hold this actor in your mind as the character. That's our advantage."

Every agent at William Morris represents the entire client list. "We break down our responsibilities according to studio," explains Kimble. "That way, somebody will be responsible for every project out there at Warner Bros., Universal, and so on. We have weekly meetings, which every agent attends. We feel that by giving one individual a limited amount of coverage, he or she will become an expert on that and let the others become an expert on what they're assigned to." Thus, they become a team, with each individual a specialist in a particular area. It works especially well when a client wants to expand his or her horizons. One such challenge arose when Brooke Shields hoped to break out of her cocoon. "She was famous for years, but no one knew she could be funny," says Kimble. "The more I got to know her, the more I realized she had a very natural comic rhythm, a beautiful woman who could do a pratfall. It's hard to find those people." Believing in her ability, he took Shields to all the presidents of the networks and studios, who continued to question her comedic prowess. "I started looking into the episodic world to see if I could find an opportunity. I did. Brooke did one episode of *Friends,* which happened to air after the Super Bowl, and within a few days we had a series, now in its third year."

Another challenge for Kimble is convincing an agent in the film department to consider helping a client make the transition from television. "The hardest part is finding a logical way to cross into motion pictures, because they're really parallel worlds with different requirements. Television is about time and money, whereas in features, you have the luxury of a much longer time frame to be creative. It's a different mind set. It's very hard to find agents who can speak in both languages." But Kimble was able to convince Michael Gruber to help George Clooney make the leap. Having a nice TVQ didn't hurt, of course, and those television clients who don't have film representation at the agency are usually those who have less celebrity status.

An actor isn't likely to get an interview at the William Morris Agency through an unsolicited submission. "Literally thousands come across our desks every year. Seeing an actor in a play or through a referral is much better," offers Kimble. Even clever mailings can be annoying to this agent. "I remember receiving a gift-wrapped box at my home one Christmas. It wound up under my tree, and when I opened it there was an actor's photo and resume. I hated it. It was so intrusive." A better approach is when an actor does some research into an agent prior to an interview. "The sooner you can find out what my hobbies and interests are or who I am as a person, the better chance you have of getting my attention." That's Kimble's preference. "When you walk into an agent's office, there are clues about that person all over. Taste in art, photos of pets or family. If you're observant, it's easy. You can carry on an intelligent and interesting conversation that makes it easier on both parties."

Once you're able to get your foot in the door, the next step is to let Kimble know you're not just another starving actor. "I want to find somebody unique, because my theory is that society programs us to be alike from the start, yet the most prized possession in the world is your individuality. And I'm constantly trying to meet somebody who is valuable, somebody who is willing to break the rhythm and expose his or her soul, do the unexpected to catch my interest." He cites as good examples of actors who don't follow the pack as Anthony Edwards, Drew Carey, Lucille Ball, and Barbra Streisand. "To me, it's about being the best you can be. Streisand has validated a type of woman considered unattractive until she came along and made her beautiful." Another example is Bruce Willis, whose hairline was receding when his agent at William Morris was trying to convince the producers that he was perfect for *Moonlighting*.

Kimble believes that an actor must stay informed and know what's current—must be, as he puts it, "a citizen of the world." The actor must keep in the best physical shape possible and continue to perfect his or her craft. "Katharine Hepburn, at the height of her career, would go back to the stage every couple of years, as do Meryl Streep and Al Pacino. It's about never saying I'm as good as I can be, but always about trying to be better no matter what your level." The ultimate piece of advice Kimble has for actors is to truly question your motivation for being in this extremely fickle business. "Don't do it unless you have to!"

Patty Kingsbaker

DONNA BALDWIN TALENT
2150 West 29th Avenue, #200
Denver, CO 80211
(303) 561-1199
FAX (303) 561-1337

Not long after she began in the business, Patty Kingsbaker knew that being in front of the camera was not for her. She had that commercial "look," but the enthusiasm and drive just weren't there. Not wanting to separate from the business completely, she decided to explore the other side, working in casting and production until, in 1990, Donna Baldwin called and asked her if she'd like to work as an agent. She hadn't actively pursued that track, but she decided to give it a shot, and nine years later she's still at Donna Baldwin Talent. "Since I was an actor myself, I understand their concerns, and it feels good to be able to help those who want to expand their horizons." Not only does the Denver agency handle commercial talent, it's also a full-service facility with broadcast and voice-over departments.

Most of the work the agency handles is industrial, both union and nonunion. Clients include Coors, Hewlett-Packard, and telecommunications company US West. There's also a fair amount of local commercial work and some national spots when a company is shooting in the area. The advertising agencies in Denver are mostly local, except for J. Walter Thompson, which has been around for years. "Last year I remember having my actors book six Ford Motors spots, the only client J. Walter Thompson handles out here." And while you may think that Kingsbaker is seeking pretty faces for those commercials, she explains that the majority of talents she represents are character actors. "We represent more than 250 actors of all ages and types. In a market like Denver you can't get too specific. There are only two SAG-franchised agents in this town. We have to cover a lot of territory." Film production in Denver isn't as lucrative as the commercial or industrial fields, but occasionally a company will bring its business to the area. Kingsbaker helped place actors in *The Shining* and in the made-for-TV movies *A Child's Cry for Help* and *Asteroid,* in which she had twenty-three actors.

When Denver actors want to expand their horizons, Kingsbaker is more than willing to assist. When one of her clients, a Native-American actor, was starring in a play scheduled to open at the Mark Taper Forum in Los Angeles, she immediately called a casting director at TNT she knew was interested in him. The casting director wound up casting Larry Swalley in *Crazy Horse.* "You have to be creative," she says, "and you have to know when it's worth pursuing the long shots."

When an actor does "make it" elsewhere, Kingsbaker has mixed feelings. "Part of me knows when they're ready to go, and I support their decisions, but it's like being a parent. You're torn. An actor who wants to make a living simply can't stay in Denver." The actors who do make a good living in that city are hosts or spokesperson types, she says. "There is no feature or television production here, and there are only a few Equity theaters. Denver is more of a training ground. You probably won't be discovered here." She does cite actors with wonderful resumes moving from Los Angeles and New York to Denver, but they do it not to build their credits but to build a better lifestyle for themselves or their families. "You certainly can be a big fish in a small pond here," she admits.

Kingsbaker recommends the National Theatre Conservatory for actors who want to study in Denver. "They take eight new students a year, and those who attend are locked up for three years. Once they've completed their training, they showcase in L.A. and New York." Again she has mixed feelings about actors who participate in the program. While they're getting wonderful training, they're not available for work most of the year. "Several actors who've graduated from the Conservatory have tested the waters elsewhere and wound up back with me. It just depends on the individual." One success story is Conservatory graduate Nick Stabile, who was with her for three years before making waves on *Sunset Beach*. As for other acting coaches, Kingsbaker is very particular. "I don't think you need to destroy an actor and build the person up again, as many teachers believe. I don't think some coaches really help. Their egos get in the way."

While Kingsbaker is not an advocate of many coaching methods, she's adamant that her actors have technique. "I look for actors in the theater," she admits. "I used to go to the theater three or four times a week. That's how I built up the agency. If she's impressed when seeing someone on stage or through a headshot and resume, she'll call the person in to read. "I especially want to see good ethnic actors and actors who can work in all media: film, TV, and commercials. If I see someone with a definite strength in one area, like commercials, I may take him or her on." Because of her background in casting, Kingsbaker reads with the talent. If she and the actor agree to work together, she'll sign the actor to an exclusive contract. "I work really hard for my actors," she insists. "I expect the loyalty to work both ways."

While photographers in Denver may not be as creative and dynamic as those in Los Angeles or New York, Kingsbaker says they're adequate; but if actors come in with great videotape, there's an even better chance they'll be at the top of her list. "If you have a good demo reel, you're pretty much assured of getting through the door." And once you do get through the door, Kingsbaker knows exactly what she's looking for. "I have a natural eye for talent," she says. "I guess it's because of my years of experience. I may see something in someone that other people don't see, and later, as it develops, they'll say, 'Oh, now I understand.'"

Kingsbaker often works more in a managerial capacity than as an agent. "There are no managers in Denver," she explains. "I take more of an interest in an actor's career and development than many agents, because that's what an actor here needs." One of the ways she may assist an actor's career is in helping him or her get an agent in another city. "I set up a meeting for Brian Allan Hill with the Michael Bloom Agency when he decided to go to L.A. I got him in the door." Of course, then it's up to the actor to clinch the deal, and one of the things Kingsbaker believes can thwart the deal is an actor's attitude. "One of the major things that sabotages an actor is a bad attitude. I knew in less than five minutes that an actress who came in to see me wouldn't be someone I'd be interested in. She had this cocky attitude. She was a very good actress, but it wasn't enough. I told her I didn't think I was the right agent for her. Her response was 'Yeah, you are!' Well, the point is that no actor should want an agent who isn't behind them 100 percent."

Fear is another negative quality she shies away from in an actor. "I've seen actors walk in terrified. I'll turn them down, because I know casting directors can smell it. If they smell fear, the actor is out." How to overcome fear? "Get out in front of people and practice," she suggests. If an actor listens to Kingsbaker it only makes the bond stronger. She admires respect and honesty. "If those ingredients aren't there," she says, "there can be no relationship between actor and agent."

Andree Kisselbach

FRETLESS MANAGEMENT
70 Greenwich Street, #A
New York, NY 10011
(212) 243-7549
FAX (212) 924-6537

It's not your typical scenario: early childhood education major gives up the security of a steady job to manage musicians. But that's exactly what Andree Kisselbach decided to do. She grew up surrounded by show business. Her cousin is Mel Brooks, and her next-door neighbor was in the popular '70s group Deep Purple. "While I was in college, I kept seeing all these musicians stumbling over their own feet, not able to manage themselves, so I saw a place where I could really do something." At first, she did it as a favor for friends at Hampshire College. "Since I graduated six months early, I decided to take an internship with Zach Smith Music. Zach was from the group Scandal; he wrote commercial music. I was the one who listened to tapes and brought in the jingle singers. No matter how talented they were, they had a hard time handling the business side of things." Kisselbach's internship turned into a full-time job, and her boss encouraged her to pursue her management dreams and get paid for what she had been doing as a favor for musicians.

Soon Kisselbach had established a niche for herself in the industry. She started handling the careers of jingle singers. "I was really helping them in all areas: publicity, creating tapes, creating images, assembling their prime marketing tools, counseling them, and helping expose them to the musical community." Today she is still a unique entity in town. She is the one to whom singers flock when they need management guidance, representation, and marketing. Mostly she handles clients with whom she maintains an extensive relationship. Occasionally she'll work in a co-management arrangement if that benefits her client's specific needs. "I only handle about fifteen clients on this exclusive basis," she explains. "Because we're working so hard to expose them to the entertainment community and direct their careers, as well as handle the marketing, we're at full capacity with fifteen."

Most of her clients are members of SAG and AFTRA, since jingle singers are represented by the same unions as other performers. "As a manager, since I don't need to be franchised by either union, I can deal with both union and nonunion projects," she says. The union jobs, she admits, are more lucrative. "We don't do a lot of negotiating for pay when it comes to union sessions, because they basically all pay scale. But it's one of the best scales in the business." She receives a 20-percent commission from all adult clients.

Kisselbach doesn't limit the types and styles of voices she represents. "I truly have to believe in the voice, no matter what it is. I have a singer, Byron C. Smith, who's a multi-genre performer. When we first started to work together I helped him create a tape that really displayed many of his different styles. No one really knew what to do with him after hearing his first tape, because it's hard to convince the musical community that you really can sing many styles equally well. After quite a struggle, Byron booked a 'country' Herr's potato chip, as well as some other country spots, all of which were really well received. I decided to create a new tape that would be strictly 'Nashville in New York.' There weren't too many country singers in New York, so that made it easier. I purchased 400 bags of Herr's potato chips and packaged each one with his new 'country' cassette, hand-delivered most of them, and Byron was on his way to a successful journey through jingle singing. He has done Mercedes, Lay's, Sara Lee, and Bud Light." Another difficult sell was Joe Lynn Turner, the lead singer of Rainbow. "He's versatile; he does character voices as well as rock. But he's also a great crooner. A couple of years ago a production company was looking for a crooner for a remake of the song 'Isn't It Romantic' for Burger King. I sent my regular crooners as well as someone I called 'Person X,' because I didn't want them to prejudge him. He was up against twelve others and he booked it."

Jingle singers don't usually need to audition in person. They're either hired from their tapes, or they're booked to do a demo recording, for which they get paid. "Tapes are somewhat speculative," says Kisselbach. "You can make [the singers] sound better than [they] actually are, and you never want to do that. Once they find out you can't really sing as well as you did on tape, you'll never get another call." Kisselbach believes the ability to do jingles is a natural gift. "It's something you can't really learn. You have to be an amazing singer and really work fast in the studio. It's gotta be a complete package. People like that aren't so easy to find." Jobs, too, aren't that easy to find, she admits. "Individuals used to make more than a hundred thousand dollars on one commercial in a year and group singers could make thirty thousand per spot. Today advertisers don't want to pay that, so they get instrumentalists and overdub. It's cheaper. They also use more existing material."

Kisselbach does not accept unsolicited tapes. The agency does accept tapes four days a year; singers must call to find out those dates. She has several consultants who'll listen to the tapes and call people in for counseling. Kisselbach feels many singers can do what she does on their own. "Some just don't have the business sense and need someone like me. This business is like playing the lottery, but the odds here are better. If you have a good voice and present it well on tape, and make sure what's on tape can be re-created in the studio, just get out there and get that tape around town. Let them know you're there. Be persistent." Then she adds, "Just don't drive them nuts!"

Barry Kolker

THE CARSON ORGANIZATION
240 West 44th Street, PH
New York, NY 10036
(212) 221-1517
FAX (212) 221-1605

Like many agents and casting directors, Barry Kolker's dream was to become an actor, but as for many agents and casting directors, it wasn't happening as fast as he wanted. "It was a lot of waiting around for the phone to ring and working nights and weekends to be free for daytime auditions. When family and friends were available to get together, I wasn't, and vice versa. I guess it boils down to the fact that I didn't want acting badly enough." He got his first taste of the behind-the-scenes work while attending college. An internship at a casting office taught him that he had a knack for memorizing actors. After a brief stint as an assistant agent, Kolker landed a job at the prestigious Fifi Oscard Agency in New York, where he rebuilt the children's department and obtained his union franchise status.

His next move was to the Carson Organization, where he currently handles both adults and children. The agency's primary focus is legit or theatrical, but they also do commercial placement. They find talent at showcases, acting schools, and seminars for actors, and by referral from managers, teachers, coaches, and other clients.

Kolker's day is filled with interviewing and going through breakdowns. "I'm either meeting new actors or talking to existing clients to see if they're happy or need us to do more for them. I'm always checking to see what types we don't have and where to find them." Combined with the routine negotiating of fees and following up on payment, Kolker has little free time. "Keeping up with changes in union regulations is enough to keep any agent occupied. The rates are always changing. It's nearly impossible to stay on top of it."

While Kolker didn't start out to be a children's agent, he found he had a knack for it during his stint with Oscard. "I really liked dealing with kids on soaps. They're always needing to replace kids on those shows because the ages change all the time." He prefers the situation at the Carson Organization, where he can represent his clients even after they're no longer minors. While the agency is primarily known for its children, adults are a growing segment of its roster. "Kids, though, are more challenging than adults," Kolker admits. "With adults you usually deal with only one person, but with kids you're going through a lot of support people, like parents and managers. With kids you've got braces one year or school conflicts the next year. Plus, if kids change physically, a producer can easily replace [them]. It's harder to replace an adult."

In addition to agenting, Kolker has also done some teaching. His experience in casting and agenting, along with his acting background, has given him a solid foundation from which to draw when young actors need guidance. "At Stella Adler [a prestigious acting school in Manhattan], I taught a class where I chose to do a lot of improvisation with actors. It's very important to see how they're able to handle last-minute changes. I also answer a lot of questions actors have when they're starting out." Kolker is an advocate of training, but he realizes that not everyone can learn how to act, and talent alone doesn't necessarily guarantee success. "Actors need energy and personality. This holds true for both children and adults." Professionalism and a good attitude are also important ingredients for a successful career. "Bringing your dog to the set is a no-no," he insists. "One kid who worked on a soap brought a friend with her each time she showed up. That's bad. You shouldn't even bring a friend along on an audition, and you should never try to 'crash' an audition, because one day it may come back to haunt you."

Kolker is always looking for attractive actors of all ethnicities between ages sixteen and twenty-five. For musical theater he prefers the so-called "triple threat" performer who can act, sing, and dance. "I encourage clients with singing or dancing abilities to enhance them. I do auditions for singers, but for dancing, I prefer to see tape." All actors interested in being represented are required to do a monologue for Kolker, and he's a stickler for up-to-date pictures and resumes. He spends a great deal of time going through pictures and tapes. At home he'll read scripts for his clients, watch tapes, and return phone calls. "I've even given out my phone number on vacation if I'm involved in a negotiation."

Indeed, Kolker never knows where he's going to find a potential client. For instance, at the beach club in New York to which his family belongs, and where they filmed *The Flamingo Kid*, he found a young teenage girl he thought would be perfect for acting and gave her an interview. "I also found a man with a great look who owned a deli. I took pictures of him and submitted him for several projects. That's one of the fun parts of the job, and what makes it exciting for both actor and agent. You never know if and when you'll discover someone or be discovered yourself. Isn't that the showbiz mystique?"

Debbi Kowall

NEEDHAM METZ KOWALL, INC.
19 West 21st Street, #401
New York, NY 10010
(212) 741-7000
FAX (212) 741-7007

Debbi Kowall was a musical-comedy actress who never expected to be an agent. She attended the University of Miami to major in drama; then to make ends meet after graduating from college, she worked as a drama teacher at a local modeling agency. "That's actually where I got my first taste of what's it's like to be an agent," she confesses. "The agents in town would sometimes ask me which of my students would be good for certain projects. They'd rely on my opinion. I kind of enjoyed that."

Still hoping to make it as an actress, Kowall moved to New York, where she saw firsthand how actors were treated by some of the bigger agencies, and she didn't like it. "I met two people, one who did soaps and one who handled Off-Broadway. I was told I was too 'commercial,' which meant I wasn't right for theatrical projects. They suggested I take classes and get into a showcase. They hadn't even bothered to have me read! All this was based purely on looks." And when she asked them to recommend coaches and showcases, she says they gave her no guidance whatsoever. "Then they suggested I take voice lessons, even though I already had a vocal coach, and they hadn't even asked me to sing a note. So I said, 'You mean I could be the world's greatest singer and actress, and you don't even care? You're recommending instruction, but you won't give me any leads? They just looked at me, and I left.'"

Three years later, Kowall decided to make the switch: She'd be the one helping actors find work. "I vowed never to treat actors as I had been treated. I read everyone who comes into my office." Depending on their interest, she'll either give them commercial copy or have them do a cold read of a scene or monologue. "If I feel they're not up to par, I'll give them suggestions. I'll recommend classes and coaches I've investigated." She does her own scouting, and she'll audit showcases and check out teachers before recommending anyone to her clients. Her main focus, however, is on the actor's personality. "Actors should be flexible and not too aggressive," she warns. "If you say you only want to do film or television, that shows a rigidity that's unacceptable. You have to be willing to do student films and independents and work on soaps, whatever you have to do to build your craft and become a working actor."

Affiliated with all the unions, Needham Metz Kowall deals with film, television, stage, commercials, and print, and also represents spokespeople. Most clients are still unknowns but are what Kowall terms "well on their way." The clients who work the most are between eighteen and the mid-forties. The most difficult placement seems to be with her models. "Casting directors think of them as pretty faces who can't act, though some can act quite well. They just have to prove themselves. That's one thing we do here," she explains. "We build relationships with casting directors so that they're more willing to take a look at someone even if they're not completely sold." She likes working with models because she feels that "beautiful is in" today, and if an attractive man or woman can act, too, that's 95 percent of the battle.

If a client is primarily interested in print, Kowall suggests having a composite. "A headshot is too limiting," she says. "A composite with three or more photos is a much more effective sales tool." The format she prefers is a laser flip card with a headshot on the front and four or five alternate shots on the back. "For commercial print, they like to see a business shot, a young mom or dad picture, and an activity shot playing tennis or golf. You can also do color test shots, which are like ads shot for a magazine but done for promotional use. There are photographers who specialize in this kind of work, and if you use several, you'll get a good variety." As for video demo reels, they're not a necessity in New York as they are in Los Angeles, but if an actor has enough good material for a reel, Kowall believes it can only enhance the package.

Kowall rarely signs someone to an exclusive contract. "A lot of our clients are very loyal and want to work only with us, but it's an open market here in New York, and we have freelance clients, too. It's less common to have an exclusive contract with a commercial client in New York, but our legit actors usually sign with us." Some actors are represented in only one area, such as commercials or print; others are represented across the board. It depends on the actor and his or her abilities and desires. Kowall's major concern is that the actor handles his or her work in a professional manner. "This is a business, not a hobby. Any time you start a business, you're going to have to invest a certain amount of money—taking pictures, taking classes. A lot of people don't really take it seriously." If she finds out from a casting director that an actor behaved in an unprofessional manner, she'll immediately address the issue, and if the actor's attitude doesn't improve, the relationship will end. "You have to be dedicated to your craft and put in 110 percent. I can only open doors. You have to walk through them."

Hugh Leon

COAST TO COAST
3350 Barham Boulevard
Los Angeles, CA 90068
(323) 845-9200
FAX (323) 845-9212

Hugh Leon grew up in the business as a child actor on Broadway for years before coming to Los Angeles to do daytime drama. Finding it less than satisfying, Leon returned to school, graduating from UCLA with a degree in communications. Wondering whether to return to the acting arena, he decided to spend some time getting to know the inner workings of talent agencies, of which, he admits, he wasn't enamored. He interned at the Bobby Ball Agency as a commercial assistant and found it more to his liking than he expected. Soon he was a full-fledged agent. "With my background as an actor, it didn't take me long to learn the technical end," he explains, adding that the agency business took him from one venue to another until he finally landed at Coast to Coast three years ago.

Housed in a former law office whose library of legal tomes still greets every visitor, Coast to Coast handles between 700 and 800 clients in their commercial department alone. They also represent film and television actors, children, sports figures, and writers. The primary requirement to be considered for representation in the commercial department is what Leon calls a marketable look. "People always ask me what that is and whether they have it. It's really difficult to answer. It's based on your instinct, whether you feel that person can be sold commercially. If [a person has] that 'average actor' look, there are just too many people like that. You have to fit a 'type.' Plus I need that actor not only to be able to carry the copy with a good, solid read, but also to know how to handle commercial versus theatrical copy." Actors should also be able to take direction well. "I'll ask actors to read a piece of copy two or three different ways to see how flexible they are." He also wants an actor who takes the business seriously; someone for whom commercials are a priority, not merely an alternative to waiting tables.

Personality is important to Leon, too. "I want to see an enthusiasm. They have to be relaxed, know how to talk, to click with me. They may have lots of talent and be good looking, but if I can tell they're going to be a pain in the ass or high maintenance, forget it." He's also adamant that, prior to coming in for a meeting, the actor has done his or her homework and found out something about the agency, whether from other actors, a publication available at Samuel French, a teacher, or a casting director. "And when you do come in and are offered representation, don't just say yes because I'm inviting you to come aboard. You have to feel you have a

Hugh Leon 97

connection with me and the agency as a whole. You have to have trust in your agent before signing." Lots of agents, he warns, will sign an actor and rarely send his or her photos out. "I tell all my clients, if I take you on, you'll be submitted for everything you're right for."

Leon finds his clients through referrals, showcases, and theater. "Pictures that come across my desk really need to blow me away before I'll call someone in from a photo alone. Half the time actors will come in and not even look like their picture." If an actor has certain marketable skills, such as the ability to speak several languages or to use a TelePrompTer, that might be reason enough for Leon to give closer consideration. If you're a minority, you're more likely to perk his interest than if you're a Caucasian female in your twenties or thirties. "It's just that there are so many thirty-year-old Caucasian women and not enough roles. They're tougher to pitch. I already have a full load." Character actors, on the other hand, are a hot commodity. "If you're funny and unique, an ad agency won't find anyone else like you. That's the kind of person I want to represent." Minority actors have better odds of being called in for an interview. "The ad agencies are always looking for fresh faces," he says. "They see the same actors over and over, and they want to see new Hispanic and Asian talent."

Commercial classes and workshops are highly recommended by Leon and the other agents at Coast to Coast. "Actors auditioning for commercials need to know the process. They're going to walk into a room without anyone there, like a casting director, to guide them. They're going be stuck in front of the camera with a board to read from, and they better be prepared! You may not realize it, but a slate [stating your name and agency] is as important as a read. You have to give them something to remember you by." A good acting class also teaches the actor how to understand the nuances of a commercial and how to pitch the name of the product. "My best advice is to take the copy, go outside the room, put it into your own words with your own attitude and pretend you're telling it to a friend. Once you get comfortable with that, you go back to the written dialogue and deliver it on camera." Leon recommends Carolyne Barry, and Stuart Robinson's classes. If you're just starting out, he suggests Tepper Gallegos for basic technique. "And most casting directors run intensive workshops that are great opportunities for actors not only to learn something, but also to get to know people who may be able to get them work." Among these are Michael Donovan, Jeff Hardwick, the Diviseks, Michael Lien, and Megan Foley. "No matter how many commercials you've done—and I've done more than 100—you always pick up something new at these workshops."

Leon has a word of warning for actors: Be nice to everyone, because you never know whom you're meeting. A case in point: Leon was at a showcase in which a client was performing. After the show there was a buffet. "I'm standing in line behind a guy who was in the showcase and his girlfriend. They were running out of food. I look down and say, 'Oh, there's not much left, is there?' And his girlfriend says, 'Oh, don't worry about it. We'll make sure we save you some.' And the guy says, 'Yeah, right! I don't think so.' He took the rest, threw it on his plate and walked off." Leon asked his client afterward who the actor was. "She tells me he was really looking forward to meeting me after the show. He's looking for an agent." Leon laughs. "I asked her to do me a favor: Go over and tell him who I am. She did. And I watched his horrified reaction. Later I walked by and said, 'Appreciate the food.'" The moral of the story: You never know!

Leanna Levy

CLI
843 North Sycamore Avenue
Los Angeles, CA 90038
(323) 461-3971
FAX (323) 461-1134

Comfort is of primary concern to Leanna Levy, not only for herself and those who work with her, but the comfort of her clients, with whom she has a great deal of empathy. "They need a safe haven they can come to after an audition, where they can have a cup of coffee and relax. We make it so comfortable, we often get thank you notes from actors we've rejected, because they appreciate the homey atmosphere we set." Levy's commercial agency has been situated in a cozy Hollywood cottage for nearly two decades, and she's particularly proud of her little patio garden, adjacent to the reception area, adorned with a variety of plants. "You see these cactuses?" she asks. "I had a friend when we first opened who had a wonderful greenhouse. She insisted I had to have plants, so she drove her little station wagon over here one day with about fifteen plants and started me off. They're still alive and kicking." As is Levy, who bought her partner out about ten years ago and has been operating the agency with Richard Ohanesian, her on-camera agent. Levy works primarily with voice-over actors.

It's important to the CLI team that actors drop by on a regular basis. "You can't help actors who just disappear. Not only do we think they may no longer be available for auditions, but we think they're not interested. It's 90 percent their career. We only take 10 percent. So if we don't hear from an actor after a month, it's out of sight, out of mind, so to speak." CLI needs to know if you've changed your hair color, grown a mustache, lost weight, and so on. "It's pointless for us to submit photographs of an actor with long hair if you have a crew cut. It doesn't reflect well on us. We need the right ammunition to do our jobs effectively. So you should keep in touch!" Levy recalls being chastised by a casting director for not telling her that one of her clients had green eyes. It happened to be a pair of colored contact lenses the actor started wearing to auditions, but that's not what it stated in her resume. "I need to know any changes, no matter how trivial you think they are. If you learn Spanish or take up the guitar you may not think we care, but we do. What if someone suddenly asks me if I have a client who plays the guitar, and you never let me know? It's vital to your career."

CLI is considered a boutique agency, with fewer than 500 clients in the on-camera and voice-over departments combined. "I chose the commercial end of the business because it's what I know. It's quick, and it's what I like best. I put out a breakdown on Monday, by Wednesday there's a callback, and by Thursday we have a booking. My problem is I'm impatient. I want to do it now. It would be hard for me to talk about a movie that's going to film next season. It's just not my style." Her style also prevents her from submitting half her client list for an audition. "I'd rather send one or two clients if they're right on the money and book the job." Many of her auditions come directly from the CDs and tapes she submits. For instance, one of her spokesperson clients, Ken Kurtis, has been hired because of his public television pledge break clips Levy keeps on hand for such occasions. She'll also submit voice-over tapes to agencies or casting directors, and if they like what they hear they'll often book the actor sans audition.

You have to be careful with tapes, however. Levy learned her lesson when she signed an actor from his audio tape. "It was wonderful, and I sent him out the next day, but he couldn't read the copy. He couldn't live up to his tape; it was completely overproduced." She never again assumed a demo tape represents the actor's true ability. She also has mixed feelings about the recent trend toward online casting, which she feels may or may not reflect the person behind the photo. "There's a story going around about a search for an Orson Welles lookalike for a feature film. The producers apparently hooked into one of these online services and found a man in Idaho and brought him in to do the movie. Because he looked right." Levy admits some of her clients get jobs primarily because of their looks, but she feels the majority of the bookings come about because they not only have the right appearance, but they're good actors.

With some 184 commercial agencies competing for jobs, Levy realizes that whether or not she approves of computer casting, it's the future. "At this point it just seems to be double the work for us," she laments. "We have to take the time to punch in, hook up, boot up, and whatever to get online, and then submit by mail as we have done for so many years, because there are casting services that aren't yet online." It's one of those inconveniences that arise during any transition, but Levy is aware that online casting will eventually supercede the traditional approach. One thing an actor should be aware of is his or her "type," so that if you do appear online, you know under which category to list yourself. Levy rolls her eyes when she recalls asking a young casting director to assist her in finding an actress. When she suggested a young lady, Levy asked for her prototype. "She had no idea what I was talking about. So I said, 'Do you know an actress who would fit her category whom we can look up in the Player's Directory?' She mentioned a name, and I asked her which category she'd be under. She said, 'Well, probably ingenuies.' I said, 'Excuse me?' And she repeated the word. I said, 'You mean *ingenue*?' She answered, 'Oh yeah, whatever.'"

Those are the frustrations Levy deals with that sometimes have her climbing the walls. But then there are the really terrific moments that keep her glued to her career. "I have a client who was in her early seventies at the time. One day she asked me if I'd like to meet her mother. I was a little taken aback, but I went out to the car to be polite. Here was this wonderful, sweet-looking lady who was eighty-nine years old. Immediately I asked her if she wanted to do commercials. She was so excited." Her daughter went home, took some Polaroids, and brought them back. Within a few days Levy happened to get a call for a woman over eighty for a Western Union commercial. "I submitted the Polaroid on a piece of stationery with a note attached: 'Please consider.' She booked the job and made thirty thousand dollars!" What thrilled Levy more than her 10 percent? "Every time we sent her a check, she called to say thank you."

Terry Lichtman

TERRY LICHTMAN COMPANY
TALENT AGENCY
12216 Moorpark Street
Studio City, CA 91604
(818) 655-9898
FAX (818) 655-9899

Ever since she was a kid growing up in small-town Western Pennsylvania, Terry Lichtman has been attracted to show business. "I'd run and get the Sunday *New York Times* and circle the shows in the theater section I wanted to see. I just loved the theater!" She would have been a casting director if she had had the chance, but without experience it was difficult. "I couldn't even type. So becoming an agent was the next best thing, and that's what I did." Twenty-three years later the Terry Lichtman Company is going strong, along with Glenn Salmers, her partner for the last two years.

The work is divided according to casting directors. "We'll choose the casting directors we each want to cover," Lichtman explains. "And sometimes we'll change off just for variety or if we feel that someone needs a fresh approach. We make all our decisions based on what's best for our clients." The agency represents both new and established actors. "We probably take on too many developmental people, but it's a challenge. If we sign someone new, we try to introduce them to the appropriate casting offices where they'd most readily get work. We love it when they hit." Recalls Lichtman, "I was just getting started as an agent when I took on a brand new, a wonderful character actor. He didn't work much his first year, but when I saw the breakdown for a major studio film it was like they had written the role for him. I was very excited. The casting director would only set up one client. He was the second actor they signed. It was all downhill following that success."

As is the case with so many rising stars, the actor left Lichtman for a larger agency, which limited him in his choices. "[The agency] turned down a lot of roles, because they didn't feel [the roles] were large enough. He finally came back after making the rounds." Almost immediately, she says, the actor received an offer for a role on a hit series that worked only one day. "He was reluctant to take it, but I advised him it would be a good move since the production company was very creative and would bring him back if the chemistry was right. It was. At the end of the season they made him an offer as a series regular," proving that it's not the size of the agency that matters, and that an actor should never get caught up in his or her own PR. "Just because an agent turns down a role, saying it's not big enough, doesn't mean the casting director is going to think more of that client. [Casting directors] just want to get the project cast. They're not interested in who's *not* playing the role. They're interested in who is."

The Terry Lichtman Company is small, handling only about 100 clients for film, television, and theater. Most of the clients come through referrals from managers, casting directors, and other clients. "Glenn also goes to the theater and attends lots of showcases," Lichtman adds. "It's definitely a good idea for actors to perform at showcases. We've signed several clients through them." The actor should have a good resume, and for the newcomer, training is important, although Lichtman points out that film and television are visual media, so what an actor looks like is very important. "I generally won't sign people if I'm not sure where they 'fit.' When you think about television, if they have to hire someone to work the next day, the person has to look the part right away. If they want a moving man, they need a big, burly guy." She apologizes, but stresses that it's her responsibility to fill the needs of the casting director. "We don't create the market; we service it."

The decision to sign someone is a collaborative effort at the Lichtman agency. Prior to making a decision, the agents will view video composites or ask the actors to do a scene in their office. "They shouldn't do scenes that are so familiar you tend to compare them with the original," she cautions. Nor should they do the classics. "They should do a scene that's really close to how they'll be cast. Write your own, if you have to." Just keep it short, and forget the props. As for 8x10s, Lichtman says it's okay to use black-and-white lithos rather than photos, because they're less expensive. When she submits an actor's photo for a particular role, she's very careful. "I have my reputation to think about. Casting directors trust me and call me for ideas. Even if an actor thinks he or she is perfect, I won't submit if I don't feel the person's really right for the role."

On the other hand, if Lichtman believes in a client, she won't give up when the right job comes along. "There was this twenty-one-year-old guy who wasn't even in the union. He was so cute. We signed him and submitted him out for a lead in a pilot we thought he was perfect for, but the casting director never returned my calls. I finally talked to the assistant, who oddly enough had gone to high school with the actor and said he was way too old for the role." Lichtman didn't give up. "I went to a brunch the following week, and who was there but an agent from William Morris who was representing the package. He told me they were pulling their hair out looking for the right actor. He asked if I had anybody." Lichtman told him about her client for whom she couldn't get an appointment. The next day he got the audition. "And that was it! He got the lead in the series, and the assistant casting director lost his job." It's always a matter of perseverance, she says. "I'm shocked when someone says yes immediately; they always tend to say no initially. I don't take it personally. I just keep the pressure on."

It's important for an actor to evaluate where he or she fits into the business, says Lichtman. "Nobody's born with credits, but at a certain point in time, you have to figure out where you fit in terms of type, and you shouldn't fight the flow. If you're not a leading lady, don't pursue it. Find out if it's acting or stardom you want. There are opportunities for actors, but it's a lot harder to be a star." If an actor isn't getting jobs, it's easy to blame the agent. "I think there's a lot of agent-bashing out there," says Lichtman, "and I only wish we had that much influence. We don't. The competition is just too tough. As agents we are one factor, but we're certainly not the whole enchilada."

Lisa and Adam Lieblein

ACME TALENT & LITERARY
6310 San Vicente Boulevard, #520
Los Angeles, CA 90048
(323) 954-2263
FAX (323) 954-2262

You don't often find husbands and wives working at the same talent agency, let alone running one. But Adam and Lisa Lieblein have managed to establish themselves as a very successful agent team in Los Angeles. Acme Talent & Literary is considered one of the best boutique agencies in town, even though it has only been around for seven years. The Lieblens set up shop after successful careers working for others: Lisa at Triad and ICM and Adam at agencies and production companies. Prior to establishing Acme, the couple ran a large networking group that included talent from almost every corner of the industry. From that support group, the Lieblens established close ties with many actors who, not unexpectedly, signed on with Acme as soon as it opened its doors.

Their basic philosophy is that they're nice guys, and they prefer having nice guys as clients. "From the beginning we decided we'd only hire people we like and to whom we can relate. We insist that all our employees have to be pleasant in order for us to hang out with them twenty hours a day, which we often do." Adam is only half kidding. The days are so long at the agency that even the couple's pet Maltese considers Acme's San Vicente Boulevard office a second home. But despite the long hours, the Lieblens try to minimize the stress that is generally a natural outgrowth of the business. Part of what makes this work is their "nice guy" approach. "At other agencies," Adam explains, "the corporate ladder is so clearly defined, people have to withhold information so they can climb it as quickly as possible. Here we create an environment where everyone benefits from everyone else's success, and we're encouraged to share information."

Unlike many other talent agencies, Acme encourages feedback from actors, and while this doesn't mean actors are free to call every day with a list of roles for which they want to be submitted, the company does ask its clients to provide any pertinent information or contacts that may assist agents in obtaining job prospects. "We have them fax us if they hear about something for which they feel they should be submitted," Lisa offers. "Sometimes an actor will tell us about a friend who's going on an audition and who's usually head to head with our actor. I'll get on the phone and make sure to get the actor an appointment." She recalls a client who booked the series *In The Heat of the Night* by employing the Lieblein system. "She had done a guest-starring role on the show and asked the producers if she could be called in again. They said their policy excluded actors from being on the show twice in the same season. The day after her episode aired, however, there was another great part she really wanted to do. She begged me to submit her, certain the director would let her audition. So I tracked him down in Tennessee. Within a half hour, the casting director called back and said, 'I don't know who the hell this woman is, but I gotta get her in and put her on tape for the producers.' She booked it!"

Acme's dynamic duo says the two things they're seeking in actors are spark and talent. "If they can come into our office and light up the room with their personality," says Adam, "these are the people who'll likely do the same in a casting director's office." Talent is very subjective, according to Lisa, but if somebody gives her the chills during a monologue, she's sold. "If they can get me to lean forward to watch them more closely during that monologue, when I'm on the phone to the casting directors I'm going to have that same feeling to transmit during my pitch." Monologues are essential at Acme. "Everyone being considered for theatrical representation has to do a monologue for us," Adam explains. "If they have a tape we'll watch that, too, but it's not as important."

For commercial representation, Adam has another approach. "I give everyone twenty pieces of copy with which I'm very familiar. I ask them to present them with their own unique flavor, whatever they think will sell that product." Adam also holds what he calls "Super Saturdays" or "Super Sundays," at which he'll see up to 100 actors. These marathon meetings are exhausting but productive, according to Adam. "Everyone I've taken on from these auditions has booked."

Trying to get in to see the Lieblens other than through a referral or open audition is very difficult. "We're working people," says Lisa. "If you're smart, you'll find someone who knows one of us and get that person to call and tell us to expect your submission. If we respect that person's judgment, we'll keep our eyes peeled." What if you don't have a connection? The submissions that get the most attention are those with an angle. "It helps if your pitch includes the name of a series you've just completed, a play that garnered good reviews, a student film everyone's talking about, or a Jack Nicholson or Richard Pryor award," notes Adam. "We're very selective. We have fewer than 200 people on our roster, including kids, and that compares to upward of 500 at other agencies." The Lieblens will only see new people in the summer and early fall. They never meet actors during pilot season, nor will they drop someone during that period, since they're aware how difficult it is to find a new agent at that time.

Currently Acme is in search of good Asian actors, musical comedy performers, and kids who can act. If you're a comic, Acme may provide the perfect nurturing environment. "Our comic department was developed by a woman who used to manage some big names, including Roseanne," Adam reveals. "Unfortunately for this agent, her apartment fell apart during the earthquake, and she moved back to Denver, leaving us with the best comics on the planet." Other performers who the Lieblens say they'll always consider are those with *Star Trek* credits. "Any episode, any version," proclaims Adam, an ardent fan. This ardor, however, did backfire not too long ago. "This one guy sent in his resume claiming he'd been on a dozen episodes, and he wanted to meet with us," Adam recalls. "We didn't recognize him, but we saw stills of him on the set and brought him in. We couldn't understand why he'd brought us a videotape. We couldn't spot him in any of the clips. We finally realized he was the guy at the console in the background. He'd been an extra for three seasons!" It's not that they have anything against atmosphere players, they just don't represent them. "So do your homework and know what agents are looking for. You'll save yourself a lot of time and frustration."

Sandi Marx

SEM&M
22 West 19th Street, 8th floor
New York, NY 10011
(212) 627-5500
FAX (212) 645-8759

Little did Sandi Marx know when she was attending New York University Drama School, dreaming of a career on Broadway, that she would be sharing her expertise as a voice-over agent with actors. But after nineteen years in the business, Marx has no regrets. "I quickly realized that if I wanted to be independent and make a living, I should reconsider my options. I had this moment at a final callback for *They're Playing Our Song* on Broadway: I could either be on stage or take a job at J. Michael Bloom [a top commercial agency]. It turned out I was half an inch too short to be hired for the show, and that half an inch gave me an incredible and lucrative career." She soon decided that her calling was to help others get acting jobs.

Marx remained with J. Michael Bloom in New York for seven years, after which she and three partners took the risk of opening their own agency: SEM&M, which stands for Schiffman, Ekman, Morrison, and Marx. "We opened SEM&M with basically a song and a prayer and not one client. But by the time we closed that first day we had four hundred!" Today it's one of the top three commercial agencies in New York with about six hundred clients on its roster. The staff boasts twelve agents, who work in on-camera, children's, voice-over, promos, and celebrities. The agency doesn't have an office in Los Angeles at this time but works closely with The Talent Group and Sutton, Barth and Vennari, as well as several others. Clients are handled on an exclusive basis. Unlike many agencies in New York, SEM&M doesn't work with freelance actors, unless there's a need for someone quite out of the ordinary, such as a Tibetan monk or Australian Aborigine.

New York is still a thriving market for voice-overs, according to Marx. The promo and animation fields are hottest in Los Angeles, she concedes, but commercial voice-overs are alive and kicking on the East Coast. "On-camera is a different story," she says. "It used to be based predominantly in New York, but in the last five to ten years it has slowly wound its way to other places such as Los Angeles, Toronto, and Florida, for several reasons: climate, unions, directors wanting to work with certain crews, and the like. We used to be very cocky here in New York about the commercial business coming solely from Madison Avenue. It's just not true anymore."

When Marx lectures to showbiz hopefuls, the most common question she's asked is how to get an agent. "From my experience," she answers, "the most successful actors I've ever found have come out of fine schools that either have leagues or audition scene night, where actors can display their talent. It's never because they look good or send me their pictures in the mail." If NYU is doing a showcase, Marx will be there. "If I see five interesting people, you can bet they're going to be in my office the next day. On the other hand, an unsolicited headshot, no matter how expensive, will probably wind up in the garbage." What Marx and her colleagues are seeking is more than the pretty face. "Can they talk? Can they act? Do they have a personality? Have they studied? It's like the old joke, 'How do I get to Carnegie Hall? Practice, practice, practice.'" She constantly reminds actors that there's always someone more talented and better looking waiting for their spot, so they have to show themselves off, no matter what it takes.

SEM&M agents keep their eyes peeled for one-of-a-kind talent. Marx recalls the time one of her partners spotted Estelle Harris [Jason Alexander's mom on *Seinfeld*] twenty years ago in a dinner theater on Long Island. "He just saw her and loved her. He started sending her out on commercials, and she was very successful right from the start." When Marx first met Wesley Snipes he was a struggling actor doing odd jobs. "He was young, adorable, and wonderfully trained, but needed guidance. We started sending him out commercially, until one day he booked the Michael Jackson video 'Bad,' in which he played the bad guy. From there on in, it was success. It happens over and over again."

With voice-overs, Marx's specialty, she needs to hear tape. "I can basically tell within twenty seconds if the tape is good, and if I want to work with the person, who has to sound real, have his or her own personality, have a voice that makes me feel this person would never steer me down the wrong path. That's most important, and there has to be something about the individual that makes me want to have him or her over for dinner." For on-camera, Marx wants a genuine person who can convince her that he or she is creative enough to invent something on the spot. "So when they're thrown a curve ball, they'll make something up so original the casting director couldn't possibly disregard them." Being original, she says, is very important. "Today's buying public is not as gullible as it was twenty years ago. You don't see 'Stepford' wives or dumb-blonde types. [Consumers] want believable people with whom they can agree rather than a hard-sell approach."

SEM&M represents actors who do a lot of New York theater. "They have a broad appeal. Many are writers; some are even rock musicians and directors. But all of them are well-read, and they're all unique." Most of their clients are already in the union, although for actors just out of school, SEM&M will work with them until they get booked and need to be Taft-Harley-ed into the union. "I always tell actors not to spend money on union affiliation unless they have to. If an agency wants you, they'll work with you until the union requires that you join." That's not to say the agency works on nonunion projects; it doesn't, although its agents will wait patiently until a newcomer books his or her first job. "It's almost a joke, but we'll sometimes wait three years for an actor to get his or her first commercial. We don't assess and judge them because they don't book. If they have a drug problem or are perpetually late for appointments, that's different; they're out. But we'll stay behind a hard-working actor whether or not they're making money. It's really not about that. It's about faith."

What disturbs Marx about actors are the chips on their shoulders that they often carry out of insecurity. "It just doesn't fly with me," says Marx. "I'm someone who doesn't care if you had to wake up early for an interview. I just want to like you, so you better be nice." And she's nice to her clients. If an actor is in the neighborhood she's happy to have him or her come in and have a sandwich. "That doesn't mean I want you coming in and chiding me because I sent you on twelve auditions in two days. Spending time with and learning more about clients is what I enjoy. We may suddenly realize an actor can do a wonderful Spanish accent or have great comedic timing. It can be quite enlightening."

While Marx enjoys actors paying visits to the office, she abhors singing telegrams or money sent in with a picture postcard asking the agent to call. "I feel like I've stolen their money," she admits. "I don't want any strings attached. Let me decide if I want to work with you. Don't send me tea to have while I read your resume. It doesn't work. We don't like gimmicks." Once you're a client however, Marx isn't opposed to the occasional box of goodies; there's already a relationship established. "The thing we agents have to remember is that we are in a service business. We're salespeople. Actors can go anywhere. We're lucky enough to have them, and if we want to keep them, we have to keep them happy."

Carol McCormick

MOORE CREATIVE AGENCY
1610 West Lake Street
Minneapolis, MN 55408
(612) 827-3823
FAX (612) 827-5345

Minneapolis is a thriving community for actors in the Midwest. In her eighteen years as an agent, Carol McCormick has seen many clients go on to flourishing careers. She herself, a psychology major in college, didn't realize she'd have such a wonderful career in a business she knew little about until she actually started working. "A friend told me about an opening at Moore Creative. I went for an interview and was hired a half hour later." She admits she had no idea the industry was such a vital part of Minneapolis life. "It was brand new to me. I didn't know how actors found work in this town." And with over 600 actors on Moore's roster alone, there had better be lots of work! That's the number of clients the agency handles for print, modeling, film, television, theater, and voice-overs. The print and modeling department tends to get the lion's share of action in Minneapolis. "There's quite a bit of catalogue work as well as fashion runway work here," McCormick explains. "We also have a thriving industrial film community, which is always seeking actors for training films of various kinds." Radio voice-overs are another source of work for her clients through several major nationally recognized advertising agencies.

The agency, which is a union-franchised operation, has relationships with agencies in Los Angeles to assist clients determined to go further with their careers. It subscribes to Breakdown Services in Los Angeles and is aware of what projects are in the works. "We'll call those agents and see if we can get our actors in the door. They primarily seem interested in our young adult clients." McCormick says she has successfully placed several young adults in series. "We were working with an eight-year-old named Benjamin Salisbury a few years ago, whom we were able to place in Disney's *Captain Ron* with Martin Short. We submitted an audition tape. They screen-tested him. He booked it, and ever since the phone hasn't stopped ringing. It was just a matter of time before he was booked on *The Nanny,* which he did for six years." What's most impressive to McCormick is that Salisbury is still with her, although he may take some time off to attend college thanks to the trust fund he acquired through his ten years of acting. Another tape submission proved successful for client Charlie Korsmo, who portrayed Jessica Lange's son in *Men Don't Leave.* That led to a call from Disney to star in *Dick Tracy,* followed by *Hook.* Unfortunately, after those three major films, Korsmo decided to seek an agent in Los Angeles, a disappointing turn of events, but certainly not uncommon or unexpected.

The tapes McCormick sends to casting directors are usually put together for a specific audition. Her young actors generally don't have enough professional material to have demo tapes available for distribution. She says it's hard enough getting demos from her adult clients, and she doesn't require video from actors seeking representation, unlike the majority of agents in Los Angeles. "I just want to see how actors can read copy I hand them, from commercial to industrial to film, and I evaluate them that way. Most of the actors I see only have theater experience, and we're the ones who help them get more." She advises actors to get copies of their work to transfer onto a demo tape, but she says it's not easy to get them to follow through. "The only time they need a demo reel is when I'm trying to get them seen by a Los Angeles agent or when we're working with an out-of-town client who doesn't have the time to audition."

Theater is a primary force in the Minneapolis area. Aside from the acclaimed Guthrie Theater, the region boasts The Jungle Theater, which does American classics and new plays; Penumbra Theatre Company, which stages African-American plays; The Children's Theatre Company, one of the finest in the country; Theatre de la Jeunne Lune, noted for its avant-garde productions; and the Chan Hassen Dinner Theatre, which focuses on musical comedy. All these are union venues that provide excellent opportunities for actors to be seen not just by local audiences, but by industry professionals who make it a point to visit the area from time to time. "It's a great training ground," says McCormick. "The Guthrie also has an experimental wing where actors can work on less traditional material and still have the opportunity to perform at the Guthrie, even though they're not on the main stage." The Guthrie also provides wonderful classes for actors from beginners to advanced. "Their best actors coach others for a very reasonable amount of money, and I encourage my clients to study with them. The other place I send actors is to the Brave New Workshop, an improv school for actors to learn the fine art of improvisational comedy. I find that's the best tool to help actors succeed in the commercial field."

McCormick believes all her clients should keep studying. "I hate to see actors who think they know it all. There's always something more out there, and classes help keep everything in good working order from one audition to another." She believes actors need to be proactive and not expect that even the best agent in town is going to do it all for them. "They need to think about their own marketing and what they can do to enhance their own careers. Most actors here in Minneapolis who really want to succeed can find a way to make it work with a little bit of this and a little bit of that. It can be a very good life."

Roxanne McMillan

12100 NE 16th Avenue, #106
North Miami, FL 33161
(305) 899-9150
FAX (305) 899-9231

Roxanne McMillan started out as a "stage mom." Her son happened to be a talented little actor who was a member of a local children's theater in Miami. "The woman who ran the theater, Ruth Foreman, was considered the First Lady of Theater in Florida, and when she asked me to work for her, I jumped at the chance. It was brutal," she admits. "I was with her a year and a half, and then I had to quit." She and her family decided to move to Los Angeles to see if their son could make it in Hollywood. "Life was hard in L.A.," she recalls. "It certainly taught me a lot about what you need to do to be a success. It's a mixture of hard work and promptness. Taking care of business. I realized that a lot of people in this business are spoiled. When they're asked to go on an audition, they should be delighted and honored. A lot of actors don't take it seriously."

McMillan and her family decided to return to Florida when finances started running low, but at that point she had quite a bit of knowledge under her belt, and she decided to go into business for herself. Twenty-one years later she's only one of a handful of successful franchised agents in the Miami area. The agency focuses primarily on film and television, and works mostly with adults. The majority of talent is handled on a nonexclusive basis and can sign with a variety of agents. Of the more than fifty clients on the roster, McMillan says only a few have signed on an exclusive basis. "If I can't guarantee someone work, then I don't want to hold them to that kind of situation. I would never keep anybody from making money." If she spots someone with unusual talent, she'll talk about the benefits of being signed with an agent. She believes that the loyalty that comes with being represented by one agent alone carries over into a closer relationship, encouraging the agent to work harder for the talent.

Most of the jobs McMillan gets for her actors are in the winter, and they're mostly in the commercial arena. A lot of the work is national and regional, with local spots and industrials rounding out the slate. She has provided talent for several major advertising agencies that handle such accounts as the Florida Lottery, Cheerios, and Coke, as well as for films that occasionally shoot in the area, including *The Truman Show* and *There's Something About Mary.* There's also a large Hispanic market in Miami, which is growing every year. McMillan has a number of Hispanic actors who are all multi-listed with a variety of agencies.

McMillan doesn't subscribe to Breakdown Services. "Everything I do here is either by phone or fax. I hardly use the Internet at this point, although Castnet [the online casting service] is pushing to get into the Miami area." It's a relatively small market, and she knows all the casting directors. In fact, one of her clients is a casting director, which is an obvious asset to McMillan. This client doesn't always use her actors, but he certainly gives her an equal shot. Casting directors will call her to give her actors time slots for all auditions. "If someone is looking for a certain type, I'd much prefer sending the actor in person rather than just sending a photo. I don't welcome the inevitable changes that are happening in casting with online submissions and the like. It's just not as personal."

When selecting clients, McMillan says she uses her instincts. "When I'm looking for commercial actors, it's the teeth," she confides. "A great smile will make money. The advertising agencies are always looking for that perfect smile." She also looks for young people just starting out whom she feels she can groom. "I just know when I see them. It's an awareness. I feel I've been given a gift for spotting talent." She also has a wonderful reputation in town. "I'm actually known for being 'too nice,'" and sometimes people take advantage of this trait. One such episode occurred when a manager brought a client in from Orlando. The young actress needed an agent in the Miami area. "I knew she'd make it. She was terrific. I quickly became very attached to her and told everyone how wonderful she was. She started booking immediately." One day the Aaron Spelling people were in town doing a search, and McMillan set up an interview with her new client. "Someone called from New York and wanted her to come up for a read. What did my client do? She had them call a new manager she had just met. She apparently took my emotional interest in her as a sign of weakness." But she wasn't devastated by this disloyalty. "If you don't let yourself get crazy over it, other things will happen."

When meeting an actor, McMillan usually provides a piece of commercial copy and a monologue. If she and the actor agree to work together, she'll suggest that the actor study the craft at a class given by a casting director. "There are a few acting schools here, but they're primarily run by actors who've never really made it. If you're going to spend all that money, you might as well do it in front of a casting director who can get you work." She also recommends that actors set up their own little theater group to hone their skills. And while actors are busy perfecting their craft, McMillan hopes they'll keep in mind that they should perfect their attitude, as well. "I wish people in the business could remember that being nice is important, too. There seems to be an attitude problem. There's a lot of arrogance. I think we can all stand to be a little more tolerant of one another, and we can definitely use a moment to stop and take a deep breath once in a while. Let's slow down, people."

Roger Meir

E. THOMAS BLISS & ASSOC.
219 First Avenue South, #420
Seattle, WA 98104
(206) 340-1875
FAX (206) 340-1194

Roger Meir always assumed he was going to continue as an insurance salesman in Pittsburgh, but when he was one of the casualties of the company's decision to downsize, he was offered a job at a talent agency at which a friend was employed. Considering that he had never known much about the entertainment industry, Meir did very well, and two years later he was in Seattle with E. Thomas Bliss & Associates. While Seattle isn't Los Angeles or New York, Meir says there's quite a bit of commercial and voice-over work in this Northwest metropolis. Some of the major corporations that generate industrial films include Microsoft, Boeing, Nike, and Eddie Bauer. "A lot of companies outside Seattle also bring work up here. We have a very fine production community. Hewlett-Packard, for instance, comes here from Texas, and Chevron is out of St. Louis."

The full-service agency handles about 460 actors of all ages, including children, and represents actors on camera, as well as for voice-over and print. "Seattle has a very diverse community of actors. We have actors who've burned out in New York and Los Angeles. They come here looking for a totally different pace. We have Academy Award nominees and Tony Award winners, as well as classic sitcom actors such as Lauren Tewes and Peter Breck. The commercial and industrial arenas, however, are quite different from the theatrical market. Most of the actors who work consistently are in their thirties and forties. It's a much younger base in Hollywood."

According to Meir, Seattle has its share of disappointments for agents and actors. "I didn't understand it, but not too long ago I saw a breakdown from L.A. for a commercial for a major department store here in Seattle. They went to L.A. to look for talent! That makes you wonder, since Seattle has the third largest community of actors in the U.S. It's quite sad, really. Another example: Our local theaters don't hire Seattle actors unless [the actors] have experience in major markets. I had to book one of our clients on Broadway to get her on stage here!" Theater in Seattle does have a wonderful reputation. The Actors Contemporary Theatre is based in Seattle, as are the Village Theatre, the 5th Avenue Theatre, and the Seattle Children's Theatre. Another theatrical organization, the Freehold Theatre Lab, is where Meir sends actors for training for voice, camera technique, and basic acting. "The instructors tend to be very strong actors themselves. The quality of instruction is phenomenal."

E. Thomas Bliss & Associates isn't always interested in experienced actors for its roster. "We've come across some pretty good actors who haven't yet built up their resumes. Basically what I do," Meir explains, "is screen each person who comes in. If an actor hasn't had any training, I'll probably pass, since representing an actor is a huge expenditure of time and effort. But if someone starting out walks in with a really great look and can give me a very natural read on a piece of commercial copy, I may consider him or her and recommend additional training." This especially holds true for children. "We had this seven-year-old go out on his very first audition for an Oscar Mayer national spot and book it. Right now he's got about eight commercials under his little belt."

Most of the film work in Seattle is nonunion. "A union actor has a hard time making it here," Meir admits, blaming the city in part for the lack of big-budget work. "There was a period about ten years ago when this city was riding high. Unfortunately there were only a few agencies with small client lists for a long time. The agents didn't have much experience. Producers were not getting the kind of service they needed, and they were getting attitude on top of that. They had to bounce around from one agent to another to get enough variety. They saw the same actors over and over, so they finally started taking their work to Portland, Oregon, to San Francisco, and back east." That's one of the reasons Meir moved to Seattle. He knew there was an opportunity to turn things around.

When actors ask Meir for advice, he tells them never to go out of town for long periods of time. He believes you can destroy your career by doing that. "Once you've built up your reputation and then leave, people forget about you and move on." Actors, he adds, should never cancel a booking at the last minute. "I've seen actors walk off the set because of some political squabble. That's not professional. One of my actors walked out because she had to hold a hot dog. She was a vegetarian. She didn't have to eat it, just hold it!"

E. Thomas Bliss has recently opened an office in Los Angeles. "It's what we call the back-door method. Casting directors won't look at a submission from Seattle necessarily, but if we have a Seattle actor we know is competitive, we'll submit from L.A. to make sure he or she gets a shot. One thing we keep in mind at all times is that we're working for the actor, and not vice versa. Some agents forget that, and it can cause tension between an actor and agent." Meir sums up his philosophy: "We're all in this together. Let's make it work."

Marilyn Scott Murphy

PROFESSIONAL ARTISTS
321 West 44th Street, #605
New York, NY 10036
(212) 247-8770
FAX (212) 977-5686

Marilyn Scott Murphy was a child actor who started acting at the age of ten and performed in nine shows before graduating from high school. In college she majored in speech and English, and obtained a teaching certificate from the state of New York. While in college she continued with her acting career. She was thrilled to be cast in the musical premiere of *I Remember Mama* in Buffalo, New York. Unfortunately, the pre-Broadway tryout never made it out of Buffalo. She moved on to Chicago, followed by Minneapolis, but her acting career came to a temporary halt when she arrived in Los Angeles. "The problem was my timing," she confesses. "I was in Los Angeles in 1980, when the actors, writers, and directors were all on strike. There was no work. So I took a job managing a restaurant. I thought I'd lose my mind, despite how wonderful the restaurant was."

Marilyn Scott (her stage name) decided to get back to the stage and New York. She did five shows in one year, mostly in Ohio, but the gypsy life was an emotional strain. She had an opportunity to help Jay Binder open his now highly successful casting office. It was quite by accident that she ended up working at an agency. She responded to an emergency phone call from her agent to fill in for the receptionist who went out to lunch and never returned. That was the beginning of her long association with her business partner, Sheldon Lubliner. In 1986, the two friends opened Professional Artists. "Having suffered the difficulties that come with an acting career, I feel perfectly suited to help guide the struggling actor."

Professional Artists handles about eighty-five signed clients and about one hundred others who freelance. They deal only with film, theater, and television, leaving the commercial end to other agencies. They primarily find their clients on stage, in performance, or by referrals. A small percentage does get selected from unsolicited submissions. There are also more unusual discovery situations. "We booked John Cameron Mitchell into *Big River* after spotting his picture in *American Theatre* magazine; and once, Jay Binder and I overheard a couple of young actors talking in a restaurant. They were so intriguing that Jay auditioned them the next day. Lance Lewman landed the role of Romeo."

If an actor is called in with whom Murphy is not familiar, she'll have him or her prepare a monologue. "I prefer to hear standard pieces," she explains. "If an actor writes it, it better be really good. The trouble with new material is I may pay more attention to the writing than to how the actor is delivering it." The most important part of the interview for Murphy is the connection between actor and agent. "I believe an agent is an extension of the actor. It is essential that the agent and actor see eye to eye regarding the actor's needs and skills. A distorted vision serves no one's best interests."

To help student actors get their bearings and find a place for themselves, Murphy uses *Theatre World* as a reference guide. She suggests looking through the books to find characters that seem appropriate: "Look up the actors who played those roles, read about their careers in the biographies in the back. It's a good way to become theatrically literate and an expedient way to find monologues." A good exercise, she suggests, is for actors to write character descriptions or breakdowns of one another. "It's remarkable how particular personality traits dominate the descriptions. It helps actors understand how others perceive them."

Murphy also encourages actors to see a lot of theater, film, and television. "See as much as you can, educate yourself, and don't rely on others to do it for you. If you're just starting out, participate in everything. Get into showcases, test your communication skills by being in front of an audience. The audience will teach you what choices are effective. Volunteer to be an usher or work for film festivals. Get involved." It helps to be in the union, because agencies are franchised by the unions and are obligated to honor union guidelines. Agents don't work on nonunion projects; however, nonunion actors can be submitted with the understanding that if they book union jobs, they must become members.

Murphy enjoys helping actors succeed. If her client has signed with the agency she'll devote whatever time it takes to help the actor land the job. "I see our office as a support center, a place to get grounded," she explains. "Personally, I'm attracted to actors who are self-sufficient and self-motivated. I prefer to help someone rather than baby-sit." In other words, if you need your hand held, she suggests getting a manager. "I feel strongly that the business is so competitive, an actor must develop inner strength in order to survive. An actor who is too dependent is at a psychological disadvantage. In acting, as in life, it's important to assume as much personal responsibility as possible. As an agent, I feel I am responsible *to* my clients, not *for* them. My ideal client has initiative, conviction, talent, skill—and some luck."

Paula Muzik

THE GEDDES AGENCY
1633 North Halsted Street, #400
Chicago, IL 60614
(312) 787-8333
FAX (312) 787-6677

8430 Santa Monica Boulevard, #200
West Hollywood, CA 90069
(323) 848-2700

Does this sound like a scene from a Hollywood film? Young lady, just graduated from college, celebrates her twenty-second birthday job-hunting at a major television network. Can't find the employment office. Gets on the elevator. Strikes up conversation with gentleman who just happens to be looking for a secretary. She gets the job! Too serendipitous to be real? Well, that's how Paula Muzik got her first job in casting. Originally from Chicago, Muzik received her degree in television and broadcasting from Arizona State and decided she wanted to begin her career in Los Angeles. Three years after getting her feet wet at ABC-TV, she decided to return home and tackle a new area: film. "That's when I got reacquainted with Ann Geddes, whom I had met in Los Angeles a few years back. She asked me if I wanted to be an agent. I said, 'Oh, okay,' and that's what I've been doing for the last sixteen years."

What Muzik prefers about agenting is the closer relationship she has with actors. "When I was casting, I was basically shepherding actors back and forth to producers, whereas now I can work with actors on a daily basis, helping them develop their careers." And surprisingly enough, there is a lot of work in Chicago in theater, television, and film. "Because of the quality of theater here in Chicago, we have casting directors come out from New York and L.A. looking for talent," she explains, "not to mention the improv groups such as Second City, which bring all the comedy folks out this way." While Muzik resides in Chicago, she still considers herself a Los Angeles agent. "It's an odd situation, but most of what I do is based on the West Coast." The Geddes staff in Los Angeles features five agents who concentrate on television, film, and theater. In Chicago there are four agents; it's more diversified and includes a voice-over department, as well.

Muzik has an affinity for actors. "For me particularly," she says, "I have a strong knowledge of theater, since I've been doing it for sixteen years. It's rare to hire an agent immersed in theater, especially in L.A. I really listen and hear what an actor tells me he or she wants to accomplish beyond making money. As they get older their needs change, and it's important to be able to interpret what the actor is saying and move within that sphere to help them ultimately achieve their career choices."

A perfect example of an actor realizing his dream is Dennis Farina who came to the agency almost twenty years ago as a detective on the Chicago police force. "When Dennis first came to us, at around forty, he'd do anything," Muzik admits. "He did commercials, even extra work. He just wanted to get in." He finally started doing theater, and because of his unique look, producers would hire him for small roles in films. "Those small roles turned into a week; a week would turn into a couple of weeks. Eventually he had full-blown movie deals." Farina was also fortunate to have met Michael Mann through a police colleague and been cast in the movie *Thief.* He was then chosen to costar in *Manhunter* with Bill Petersen. "It was awkward timing," says Muzik of Farina's feature film opportunity. "He was one year short of his police pension, and he decided simply to walk away from the force rather than risk the chance of putting his career on hold." At least his decision was a rewarding one for Farina.

Muzik finds most of her clients through referrals, although she claims she opens every submission that comes across her desk. A good photo may attract attention. "You know what a good picture is?" Muzik asks. "It isn't about the photo at all. It's about whether the photographer has been able to capture the soul of the actor. A good photo tells me right away who this person is." A good picture, to Muzik, enhances the resume, which is vital when being considered for representation. "It's really a package for me, because I read the resume carefully. Even if someone doesn't have a lot of credits but has had exceptional training and has a great look, I'll bring the person in." As for that vital training, Muzik would rather see an actor come out of a four-year college program than simply have taken acting classes in town. "It's a structured environment that provides a lot more focus. Even though college doesn't often focus on film or television, it's theater training that's the most important. Once you can do that, you can easily learn the other stuff."

It may seem like a contradiction, but Muzik believes there are two types of actors who succeed: those who devote all their time to their career, becoming almost obsessive about it, and those who have a life outside acting and bring to their performance the multitude of experiences they've accumulated over the years. "It can work either way," she believes. But she also insists that actors continue perfecting their craft. "The competition is worse than ever, but casting directors aren't increasing the numbers they call in for an audition. A casting director usually brings in six people per role. That's six out of six million! If an actor complains of being rusty because he or she hasn't been on an audition in a long time, I say, 'It's your job not to be rusty. Figure it out.'"

Muzik doesn't mince words. That, she claims, is one of her strong points: letting actors know exactly where they stand and what they should be doing to improve their chances of success. "When I first met Michael Shannon," Muzik recalls, "he was sixteen. He had just arrived from Kentucky. This kid had more talent in his little finger than most have in their entire body, but as a teenager he was maddening. He was impossible to locate, and he never brought in his pictures and resumes when we needed them." Shannon dropped out for a year, and when he decided to get back into the business, he knocked on Muzik's door. "I said to him, 'Michael, I'm too old and too tired to work on your career by myself. You have to help me.' He promised he would, and he did. For the last four years he has been building his career and [went on to star] in *Killer Joe,* [a hit] in New York."

Muzik suggests that actors really question their motivation. "I think actors need to figure out if their careers are working for them. Are they able to get up every day and say they're happy in their chosen profession? If the answer is no, then it's time to leave. I've watched too many actors plugging away for years and years, never really going anywhere. It's sad, because they often turn bitter. If you don't love it, leave it. Life is too short."

Christopher Nassif

CNA & ASSOCIATES

Agents: Ellen Drantch, theatrical; Adrienne Spitzer, theatrical; Stephen Rice, theatrical; Patrick Collar, commercial; Courtney Hanlon, commercial; Wendy Morrison, commercial; Simon Schwarz, print

1801 Avenue of the Stars, #1250
Los Angeles, CA 90067
(310) 556-4343
FAX (310) 556-4633

With the large number of theatrical agencies in the Los Angeles area, it's helpful to know which ones are open to new faces and which are adamant about having only experienced actors on their rosters. Some, like CNA & Associates, fall in between. While CNA deals primarily with experienced actors with extensive resumes, the agency is open to fresh faces, as long as they come highly recommended from a reliable source.

Christopher Nassif, who founded CNA in 1982, is always on the lookout for hot young talent. "Most of them come from our New York affiliates, who send people out here all the time. If the actors have charisma and an ability to act, we'll get behind them and take them to a very high level."

CNA has thirteen agents representing theatrical, commercial, young people, writers, directors, below-the-line, and composers. While the agency represents a large number of people, each department is relatively small. There are only sixty-five to seventy actors in the theatrical department, for instance, which would give it "boutique" status if that were the only department in the agency.

"We drop a few clients every year, and a few drop us," admits Nassif, "but because we don't take on a lot, it's pretty stable around here." If there's real talent knocking at the door, however, he'll always consider an addition. "Believe it or not, real talent is hard to find. Even if an actor appears to be talented, what's inside making them tick may not be deep enough to take them for the long haul. I get a gut feeling about that. In a roundabout way, I always ask the actor to explain his or her reason for acting. If it's to be a star, to sign autographs, or have the ego stroked, we're not interested, because most of the time, that person won't have what it takes to sustain a career. What I want to hear is that what they love doing is being an actor."

That's why Nassif likes to see theater credits on a resume. "That lets me know the actor is serious. They don't care where they're acting. They just love the art. You don't find a lot of actors like that. Most are pursuing the field for the wrong reason." Nassif knows whereof he speaks. He was an actor for a brief time, turning to the agency business when he realized he was better at guiding others and networking. At the age of twenty-two he found himself "fathering people twice my age," including Delta Burke, whom he placed on *Designing Women,* and Dorien Wilson, one of the former stars of *Dream On.*

Now, after years of experience and a client list that includes Ed Lauter, Olivia Hussey, Will Friedle, and Michele Greene, Nassif still believes that agenting is about "fathering" clients. "I'm like a manager," he says. "We worry about our clients. We want to take them to stardom. The large agencies put tons into decor. The actors look at that and get a false sense of security." They're also misled, he adds, by what he calls the "myth of packaging." "The large agencies say, 'Come with us. We'll package you.' Well, if you're a major star, anybody can package you. Your lawyer can package you! Look at Jack Nicholson and Harrison Ford. They've been with small agencies for years. When you're with a large agency, you're simply competing more."

That's why Nassif doesn't spend his time looking at pictures and resumes. "If we're constantly meeting with actors, we're not working for the ones we already have. We get hundreds of submissions, but to be honest, I don't look at them. Our receptionists do. If something sparks their interest, they'll let us see them." But it's rare, he confirms, that an unsolicited photo will ever get past the reception desk. His clients are there because they've been seen in the theater or through referrals, and they usually have a good reel. "If an actor doesn't have tape," says Nassif, "I'll ask them to do a scene. Forget monologues. You can have a monologue rehearsed for twenty-two years." When actors do scenes for him, Nassif wants to see both comedy and drama. "If we're going to commit to the actor, we have to know that he or she is truly committed to acting. That's not to say that we'll pass on actors who are only comfortable with comedy. We're open. As long as they have good tape that's recent, with professional material on it."

CNA will nurture new clients, helping them get their feet wet and letting them acquire more experience. Then the agency will push the actor to the next level, and Nassif does mean push. "We find that casting directors are too busy to see actors who may be perfect for a role unless you push. So we feel we're doing everyone a benefit by being aggressive and insisting they see our client. Of course, you have to be careful to push only when you know you're right." Nassif feels that casting directors actually respect an agent who'll push a good client and look down on those who don't. "They think less of them," he says. And he should know. His wife, Robin Stoltz Nassif, is a prominent Los Angeles casting director with Slater and Associates.

Nassif admits that to be sufficiently aggressive without being obnoxious is an art. "Luckily, I've always had that ability," he boasts. "Our main responsibility is to employ the actor, give him or her the opportunity. We'll do anything we have to that's legal to get the client the job!" As for the actor, his or her reciprocal responsibility, according to Nassif, is to have faith in the agent. "It's like a marriage. It's a two-way street. We all have our ups and downs in the business, and when actors feel the world owes them a living, that arrogance disturbs me. I like humility. When I meet an actor with an attitude, I won't deal with that person."

He is also unsympathetic to those who refuse to take his advice. "When people come to us, aren't they coming for advice? If they think they know it all, it won't work. I suggest they get into a good play. They balk at that. I tell them to get with a good coach. They argue. We'll drop a client if they stop listening to us. If you don't trust your agent, you shouldn't be with that agent." And he offers this additional advice: Keep a positive outlook, and know where your true allies are. "Take responsibility for your choices. If your agent has been loyal, don't jump ship to where you think the grass is greener. It's a myth. Stay with someone who believes in you. It'll make the industry a better place in which to work."

Nassif believes that it's actors who give agents power. "If you don't jump ship you won't be giving the larger agencies in town all the power. They are deal makers. We do the hardest job of selling you. We have a vested interest in you. Give us a chance."

Jean Nicolosi

WALTERS AND NICOLOSI
1501 Broadway, #1305
New York, NY 10036
(212) 302-8787
FAX (212) 382-1019

Jean Nicolosi was in charge of the theater department at Boston University until one day she woke up and realized she didn't want to be part of suburban academia any longer and moved to New York. After obtaining her Equity card, she decided acting wasn't her forte either. What to do? "What would suit my background, pay the bills, and be interesting? I had friends who were agents. They made a few phone calls, and soon I was working in an agency and loving it. That's when I decided to become an agent, and I've been doing it ever since." Nicolosi loves working with actors. "It's so creative, looking at different scripts and thinking which actors would be right for which roles. It's challenging, and it's fun."

The most challenging aspect of her job is getting actors to understand what they're right for. "It's very important to know who you are. There are people out there who don't want to accept the fact that they're character actors, not leading men or women. If we can't communicate on that basic level, there's no going forward at all. I can't represent people who see themselves differently from the way I see them." Nicolosi is very selective when it comes to representing clients. The boutique agency handles about seventy-five actors in New York and recently opened an office in Beverly Hills, where her partner, Bob Walters, is now headquartered. "We were losing clients in New York because we didn't have representation on the West Coast, so we decided to take the next step, and it's working out great."

Nicolosi is a tough negotiator. She doesn't like seeing her clients taken advantage of in the industry. She cites as an example a young actress she represented on Broadway. "Daisy Eagan, who had a starring role in *Secret Garden* when she was ten, was invited to participate in readings of new screenplays at a summer film program. They provided a stipend of only $100, which didn't include meals. At the time, Daisy was in college and couldn't really afford much, so I made sure she earned an extra fifty dollars a day for expenses. It wasn't a big deal for the program, but it made a big difference for Daisy."

Young people represent a large chunk of Nicolosi's business. The agency doesn't usually take on actors younger than fourteen, but they do handle teens and young adults right out of college. "That's the best," she insists. "We look for actors who've just graduated from Carnegie Mellon, ACT, Julliard, and the Old Globe. They're fresh and well trained, and there are a lot of opportunities, since young is very much in demand." A young lady the agency signed two years ago, right out of school, has already done two features, has guest starred on *Dawson's Creek*, and has a leading role in the Spelling television series *Charmed.*

If actors haven't received sufficient training in college, Nicolosi steers them in the direction of talented coaches. "I'm always referring clients to Kate Smith, who's based in Los Angeles but occasionally comes to New York to give a master class. She can work miracles, helping them with cold readings for on-camera auditions. The ability to handle cold readings," she adds, "is a technique, not so much a talent. If you can learn that technique and then apply your natural talent to it, you're way ahead of the game."

Nicolosi believes you're never too old or experienced to stop studying. "I went to hear Ellen Burstyn speak at a college recently. Afterward I spoke with her backstage and asked her whom she'd recommend as an acting coach. She told me she still studies acting and reads every new book that comes out about the industry. I was amazed and enlightened."

Nicolosi will rarely see an actor without a referral, although the agency receives hundreds of unsolicited tapes and photos every week. If she is interested in meeting someone who's new to the field, she'll ask the actor to prepare a scene. If "all the pieces fall into place," she'll discuss representation. She prefers, however, to have seen an actor's performance, either on stage or on screen, prior to consideration.

The agency is online. Breakdowns come across their computers every night, so by the time the agents walk into the office in the morning, they're already familiar with the day's casting notices. "Our meetings in the morning are very quick. We compare notes, and we're off submitting to casting directors." They also use the Internet for downloading sides for their actors, and if their clients subscribe to the Academy Players Directory, they can have casting directors download photos and resumes without having to take the old-fashioned route of putting them in the mail. "It's amazing what a time-saver the Internet has become," she admits.

Does Nicolosi encourage her young actors to pursue their career despite the odds? "Let me answer that," she says, "by telling you the story of a brilliant young piano student in high school. He asked his teacher if he thought he'd ever be a concert pianist. The teacher looked straight into his eyes and said no. The student shrunk under his glare and walked sadly away. Years later, at a high school reunion, the young man walked up to the teacher and asked why, years ago, he'd told him he'd never make it as a professional pianist. The teacher answered that if he had to ask him and relied on his opinion, he never would have succeeded. It's about believing in yourself, doing the work to support your beliefs, and one day it will happen if you hang in there long enough. You have to believe in your talent and not let anyone make that determination for you."

Bob Preston

CUNNINGHAM, ESCOTT, DIPENE AGENCY
10635 Santa Monica Boulevard, #130
Los Angeles, CA 90025
(310) 475-3336
FAX (310) 475-6127

It may seem strange, but with the number of talent agencies in the Los Angeles area that handle young people, there's only one that holds a regularly scheduled open call for new talent. That agency is the well respected Cunningham, Escott, Dipene Agency (CED) in West Los Angeles. Under the guidance of Bob Preston, Portia Scott Hicks, and Carolynn Cher, the children's department has been holding open calls for more than ten years, and they find them a useful tool for rounding out their rosters. "Commercial casting directors are looking for a large selection from which to pick," Preston explains. "They'll ask us to send them whomever we think may be right, so we need a lot more actors in our commercial department, and we often find those young people at the open call."

The three agents hold open calls the first Monday of every month (except holidays) from 6:00 to 6:30 P.M., in which short time the agents see between fifty and two hundred kids between the ages of four and eighteen. The procedure is simple: The kids and their parents form a line outside the office door; as soon as Preston, Hicks, and Cher arrive, they bring five kids at a time, usually all within the same age range, into the small reception area and have them stand side by side facing the agents across the room. Each child hands the agents his or her photo, which can be a simple snapshot or a professional headshot and resume. They're then asked to state their full name clearly, deliver a simple line of commercial dialogue, and leave to make room for the next group of five. It's that quick.

"It doesn't take long for us to determine who we're going to bring in for a callback," Preston says. "You know right away if the child doesn't really want to be there, and that it's the parent who's more intent on a showbiz career. If the child won't follow our simple direction or won't look us in the eye or speak up, we probably won't call him or her back." The agency isn't allowed to advertise these open calls, since it's against the rules for talent agents franchised by the Screen Actors Guild to advertise for clients. So, they rely on word of mouth, and tell those who call that instead of submitting photos it would be better to attend the next open call. They also prefer meeting a child in person, instead of just seeing a picture, which they may throw away, thereby missing out on a wonderful personality.

What the children's department is seeking at an open call depends on the roster at the time of the audition. "When we meet kids," Preston explains, "we may have a need for someone in a certain age group. We may have an abundance of kids in other age categories, so even if a child has talent, we may not be able to bring him or her in. But if that child came back six months later and a slot opened up, it might work. So it's not necessarily that someone isn't good, it's just that the timing may be off." There have, in fact, been sessions at which they've signed three out of ten kids whom they've called back, and others at which they passed on everyone. "It varies from month to month. For commercials we need a bigger roster: three blondes with blue eyes, three African-Americans, and so on. For theatrical we may only need one kid in each category. But our clients do move on. They drop out sometimes if they don't book that first or second job, and we'll have to fill the space."

There's no dress code for the open call. Kids should just be kids, the agents advise. If there's a stain on someone's T-shirt, that's okay. The only thing they ask is that the kids don't have candy or gum in their mouths, and that they're ready to talk. Indeed, shyness may be cute in other situations, but not at an audition. The more outgoing the personality, the better the chance of standing out and attracting attention. Despite the speed of the process, the three agents take notes throughout the session, and when a youngster captures their attention, his or her picture is put aside for further consideration.

Why does CED hold these open calls when other agents turn their noses up at the procedure? "There are a lot of parents out there who don't know how to get their kids evaluated for free," Preston maintains. "Lots of companies advertise about their evaluations, but they charge a lot of money. At our open calls we provide that opportunity at no cost. You'll get an answer. We'll possibly get a client, and we'll save you a lot of money." In a business that's all about talent, this is one of the few certifiable agencies that actually opens its doors, if only for a mere thirty minutes a month, to anyone with the Hollywood dream.

Mark Redanty

RICHARD BAUMAN & ASSOC.
250 West 57th Street, #2223
New York, NY 10107
(212) 757-0098
FAX (212) 489-8531

When he was in college in the '70s, Mark Redanty wanted to be an actor or director. His focus changed when he went on a field trip from Ithaca College to New York City, where he attended seminars with various alumni, one of whom was a commercial agent. "We really hit it off," he recalls, "and she ended up offering me a job as a trainee. Unfortunately, it only lasted six months, because the actors went on strike that year." It took Redanty two and a half years to find another agency job. He studied theater, but soon realized the life of an actor wasn't for him; he preferred being the middleman. "I love dealing with actors and being there when they have their successes. I enjoy the small contributions we can make by pushing the right actor someone may think isn't right for something, but we know is."

Having had some training as a youth in theater, Redanty feels he can really relate to actors and dancers. The East Coast office of Bauman & Assoc. handles film, television, and theater; and while Redanty works in all three fields, his passion is theater. "A large percentage of the work we get is theater, because that's New York. There's so much of it here." The Los Angeles office concentrates more on film and television. Some of their clients are represented by both offices, but it isn't mandatory. Agents on both coasts have to want to work for the client in order for that person to be represented bicoastally. "We like the decision to be unanimous," says Redanty. "But if it's an actor I've seen, and the other agents haven't, they'll take my word for it."

He sets up interviews nearly every day to meet new actors. When there's a group he and his associates haven't seen perform, they'll rent a studio and invite those actors to come down and audition. This usually happens twice a year. If an actor is established or has good tape, an audition isn't necessary, but unknowns are given a chance to display their talent, whether acting or singing. "We ask them to do whatever they do best," Redanty explains. "I prefer to see a monologue rather than a scene, because if you can't do a monologue and you want to be an actor, there's something wrong. There are so many people who have no training and want to act, and it's foolish. You have to learn technique." He believes the dynamics all come to the forefront during the performance of a monologue. "If you can't stand up there alone and speak the words intelligently, then you're in the wrong business."

An actor must know his or her strengths and weaknesses, according to Redanty. "I met a very sweet, cute comedienne through a manager recently," he recalls. "She seemed like she'd be perfect for a sitcom. Her resume was filled with comedic roles, and I was very interested in her. What does she do for her audition? A monologue from *Medea!* I was shocked. I was waiting for her to make us laugh, and there was this heavy monologue." He asked her why she chose *Medea*, and she explained that she wanted to show him she had range. "Unfortunately, I didn't feel her classical work was strong enough for us to represent her, so she shot herself in the foot." Actors, he says, are so afraid they're going to be typecast. "And I say you can't be typecast if you've not been cast. Do the same type of role four or five times, make a name for yourself, and then cross over and do something else."

Redanty warns actors not to give away their power. "Actors don't always realize they have most of the power in the audition room. They give it to the people behind the table, which is easy to do when they're intimidated by them. What they have to remember is that these people want you to be good and do your best work. Actors need to maintain confidence." He cites an example of an actor who was asked to do a scene a second time a different way, and as he was leaving the audition he realized he hadn't done it the way they had asked. "So I asked him if he requested another chance to read. He said he was hoping I could call and get him in for another audition. Well, that's not going to happen. If you're in the room and want to do the scene again, you have to ask."

In many ways, Redanty acts as a manager. He often assists actors preparing for a big audition, as happened during a search for the cast of a film biography of singer Ricky Nelson. "These young guys don't even know who Ricky is. They're in their twenties. So I'm explaining who he is and recommending videos to look at. It happens a lot. They're going out for a musical and want to run their songs by me to see if they're appropriate. I'll help with dress or give them insights into the casting directors if I know them, whatever I can do to help them book the job." Some actors, he says, need that extra boost. "I had an actress going out for a musical, and I happened to know that the song they wanted her to sing was originated by Ginger Rogers in a 1933 movie, which I have at home on tape. So I brought it in, cued up the song, and showed the actress what they were looking for. It really helped."

Redanty will also help his clients when it comes down to selecting who gets the all-important audition. "I'll get on the phone and push," he admits. "I'm not afraid. I have a client, Luba Mason, who [was] on Broadway as the lead in *Jekyll and Hyde,* and they didn't want to see her, because the last thing they saw her do was a completely different kind of role. They liked her but thought she wasn't right for this. I insisted, and she got the part." What bothers Redanty the most is dealing with the younger casting directors who don't know certain actors and don't put their trust in him. "Not that they have to do what I tell them, but I know these actors, and they don't. I guess trust comes with time." And most important for Redanty is that actors trust themselves. "It's about your work. If your work is good, you'll do okay. If you're an artist and make your decisions based on art, not on money or glory, you're on the right path." His passion is the artist. "Actors who forget that acting is an art form are misguided. And, as an artist, you can't stop growing. A concert pianist practices every day. The same rules apply for actors. If you pursue your art, you will succeed. That's my philosophy."

Diana Rollnick

SAMES & ROLLNICK
ASSOCIATES, LTD.
250 West 57th Street, #703
New York, NY 10107-0703
(212) 315-4434
FAX (212) 582-0122

Diana Rollnick and Mary Sames worked together years ago at Leaverton Associates in New York. Rollnick was an associate, and Sames was second in command. Shortly after Rollnick was franchised, she and Sames decided to open their own office in 1985, and they've been together ever since.

This established agency has grown to four agents, representing actors in theater, film, and television. Unlike at many other agencies, Mary Sames, Diana Rollnick, Peter Sherwood, and Tony Cloer work as a team, rather than sorting out the casting directors and studios "The way we operate, everyone knows what each of us is doing at all times." They consider themselves a boutique agency, representing between eighty and a hundred actors. The agents like to work closely with their counterparts in Los Angeles, including the Artists Agency and House of Representatives, and they're always open to collaborating with other agencies with good reputations on the West Coast. Together they keep their eyes open for well-trained, educated actors. "It's getting harder and harder to find classically trained actors, because today it seems even Broadway is star-driven," bemoans Rollnick. "When Candice Bergen decided to do *Murphy Brown*, that was when things started to change. Movie stars never did TV before."

Rollnick and company discover their talent mostly from theater and referral. "If I see someone in a show, I won't hesitate to write a note asking the person to call me if he or she is not already represented." All the agents attend showcases to ensure no stone is left unturned. "Unfortunately there are more actors than jobs, so the competition is staggering." But Rollnick isn't afraid to be persistent with casting directors if she feels her clients should be seen. All four agents do everything they can to get casting directors to the theater to see their clients. "We'll fax or call or do whatever to arrange tickets," says Rollnick. "It's not easy. Everyone is busy. I always tell my clients, if they want to do showcases, fine, but do it for yourself, not because you want important people to come. If they show up, that's just a bonus."

Most importantly, Rollnick believes, actors should devote their time to perfecting their craft: taking classes in acting, singing, and dancing. The office prefers seeing someone perform entire pieces on stage and then inviting the person to come in and chat. Rollnick recalls meeting Yeardley Smith that way. They discovered her at the Canyon Festival Theatre in Ohio. "We went to see a play called *Hitchin,* because we represented the playwright and the star. Smith was tremendously talented, and she's now one of the stars of *The Simpsons.*

One of the biggest changes Rollnick has noticed in the business is the casting of animated features. "When it first began with Disney's *The Little Mermaid,* they were always auditioning New York theater actors. When they did *Beauty and the Beast,* we represented Jesse Corti, who played Le Fou. Then *Aladdin* came along, and we had Jonathan Freeman cast as the villain, Jafar, in that movie. Since then it has been all celebrity voices. To me, that lessens the enjoyment of the film. Now, when I see the movies, instead of getting lost in the story, all I can think about is whose voice am I hearing."

Will a client get lost at Sames & Rollnick? Not as long as Mary and Diana are running the business. They're loyal to their actors, the majority of whom, in turn, are loyal to the agency. They understand that actors have to pay the rent and accept jobs that may not be related to the industry. "I would just prefer that the jobs be survival jobs, not real jobs, like ten-to-six occupations. You can't do that as an actor. You have to wait tables at night or do telemarketing or computer stuff. You have to be free during the day for auditions." What Rollnick wants actors to do from ten to six is put their efforts into their career: sending out resumes, taking lessons, going to the gym to stay in shape. "It's a business. The more knowledge and the more hunger an actor has, the better. It feeds the soul. You can't depend on anything or anyone but yourself."

David Roos

GILLA ROOS AGENCY
16 West 20th Street, 3rd floor
New York, NY 10010
(212) 727-7820
FAX (212) 727-7833

Is it possible to segue into the acting arena through modeling? Yes, but as with every other attempt to break into the business, nothing's guaranteed. If you're going to try, however, you might want to find a modeling agency that also has an on-camera department. That's the case with the Gilla Roos Agency in New York, which has been around for more than twenty-five years. Now run by Gilla's son, David, the agency is one of the most respected in the country. "I never thought I'd be running my mother's business," Roos admits. "I was a chef. I was getting tired of it, though, and when my business folded my mother suggested becoming an agent, so I did."

Roos and his employees represent actors and commercial print models. Some of the clients are covered across the board, in all areas. Others are brought aboard in a specific division, depending on their looks, talent, and experience. "Most of those we represent have an acting background," he explains. "Photographers today want people to appear to be in a real situation, as opposed to a stylized pose for ads. We call it mock print. The better our models are as actors, the more likely they are to get hired."

The agency also has a television commercial division, a children's department, and a theatrical department established in the early '80s to handle soaps, series, and features. The print division, however, is what drives the agency. Each division handles both exclusive and freelance actors and models. Roos' bailiwick is print, but he's always on the lookout for talent in each of his divisions. "I think I have a good eye," he says. "I'm not necessarily seeking gorgeous people, although if you're attractive there's plenty of work out there. In fact, actors in their mid- to late-thirties and early-forties who are good-looking yuppie types work the most. However, there's also work for real people and character types in both commercials and print." One trend he sees is toward youth. "Everything's becoming very youth oriented all of a sudden, and advertising copies society's trends. That's why I have to watch TV and read lots of magazines, just to see what's happening."

The agency acquires most of its modeling calls from photographers. Commercial casting is either through Breakdown Services, or Roos and his colleagues will get direct calls from the ad agencies. Most of their print models are freelance, with about thirty or so represented on an exclusive basis. "When I'm asked to submit for a particular project, I go through all my photos. We're really organized here. We're computerized. Our files are in order. We don't want to miss anybody." With print, an agent is often able to submit twenty people for one job, more than most theatrical agents are allowed. "I refuse to send out anyone who isn't trained. We have a good reputation. A lot of agencies call us exclusively and book our clients without auditions. I wouldn't want to jeopardize that by sending out unprofessional actors or models."

Ad agencies are often drawn to Gilla Roos' all-inclusive website. "They can do a completely interactive search for talent simply by entering the statistics. It has taken us a year to get this completed, and it's great. If an overseas client wants to book one of our people, all they have to do is get online and search. The web," Roos insists, "is going to be the future of commercial and print casting, especially print." Another trend Roos observes is toward ethnic casting. "The Hispanic market, for instance, has grown a hundredfold here in New York. I represent a lot of both Hispanic and African-American actors. Commercial print used to be very 'white bread,'" he explains. "It has become very urbanized, especially over the last five years." He also concedes that print has changed a lot in recent years; casting directors are now being hired by ad agencies to find print models and actors. "They want it real. They don't want showroom models who look stiff and unnatural."

As to whether or not someone needs to go to modeling school to become a model, Roos says it depends. "It's useful for some people, to develop poise and confidence, but I don't think most people need it. What you do need are talent and the right look. I don't recruit my talent from modeling schools." He finds his people through submissions or by running into someone on the street or at a party. "I find people every day who have no training or experience. I remember a Hispanic boxer came in one day. He had a great face. He has twenty commercials under his belt now and has been on *Law and Order*." Others who've made the transition from model to actor are Courteney Cox and Faith Ward.

Roos warns actors against trying to handle job-related problems without the assistance of an agent. "It's one of the biggest mistakes actors make. All you have to do is take one moment and call your agent. It would save so many headaches." He also feels it's important for actors to realize the symbiotic relationship between agents and actors. "The agent's job is to find opportunities for actors. As an actor, your job is to be prepared and do your work, have your headshots and resumes up to date, and represent the agency in a positive manner. I don't see enough of that. It's a two-way street. It takes teamwork."

Susan Salgado

TRIPLE THREAT CASTING
10480 Sunland Boulevard, Suite 13
Sunland, CA 91040
(818) 352-0208
FAX (818) 352-9488

If you're an actor who happens to excel in the fields of music or dancing, you may want to contact Susan Salgado, since her background is professional dance. Formerly at Bobby Ball Agency, Salgado recently opened her own Agency, Triple Threat Casting. After being discovered with her three sisters on *Star Search '91,* Salgado appeared in such films as *Harlem Nights* and *One Good Cop.* After nine years as a performer, and realizing that a petite Filipina who was no longer twenty-something wouldn't have the most dynamic career as a performer, Salgado made a wise decision: to help young talent fulfill their dreams. "I'm still attached to the business, but on the other side. Having been a performer, I can put myself in a client's place when I'm negotiating, and it helps."

At Bobby Ball, Salgado was the director of the dance, music, and choreography department, and represented vocalists and musicians both on and off camera. Musicians would be prescreened on videotape or audio tape and later brought in for a live audition, while dancers would be asked to perform at new-client auditions scheduled every other month at a nearby studio. "We [did] two hours of hip-hop followed by two hours of jazz auditions. The dancer [came] in with a photo and resume, [learned] the combination, [was] put in a group, and [performed]. If we [liked] what the person [did] in hip-hop, he or she [could] stay for the jazz portion." With a good reputation in the industry for dancers, Salgado is very selective. "[At Bobby Ball] we booked *Gepetto,* a movie of the week starring Drew Carey, which needed lots of dancers, including kids. We had a lot of clients in *Dance With Me,* and we [were] always booking commercials, live shows, and music videos."

If you have a specialty act such as ballroom dancing or pointe ballet, you'll be asked to submit a videotape. "Most of those we represent in that area have championship titles." So if you've just completed an Arthur Murray dance class, don't even bother, not until you've competed and won a few trophies.

Agents like Salgado represent dancers who perform in the preshow before the Disney film screenings; this type of variety show is booked under an AGVA (American Guild of Variety Artists) contract. Those who perform in music videos work under an industry-enforced contract through a nonprofit organization called Dancer's Alliance. "Dancers represented by agents have formed a nonprofit organization to secure rates so that dancers won't be taken advantage of financially. We collectively agree that no one will work below a certain fee, which is $200 per rehearsal day and $400 for a ten-hour shoot. We make sure they don't work under hazardous conditions and are paid for overtime."

After reviewing tapes, if Salgado is interested in seeing particular singers, she'll ask them to come in for an audition, where they'll be expected to prepare sixteen bars of music. If Salgado is sufficiently impressed, she may want to hear a contrasting song. Musicians rarely have to audition if they have good tape. "Of course I'm always seeking a performer who can do it all," she smiles. "If you can act, sing, and dance then you're a Broadway contender, and while we have lots of supporting stars and chorus people, we're always seeking leading men and women."

Salgado confesses that it's difficult to keep young male dancers from dropping out and turning to other pursuits such as sports. "We're always looking for prospective clients who love the field. We find kids at a dance school up in Fresno [in central California] as well as in San Diego and San Francisco. We judge a lot of competitions across the country, looking for new talent. If they're interested in representation they might move to L.A."

There are dozens of dance schools in the Los Angeles area, but Salgado works with only a few that she believes to be the most professional. "The Edge Dance Studio in Hollywood has a lot of great teachers, as does the Dance Center in North Hollywood and the Performing Arts Center in Van Nuys. They provide scholarships for teens and young adults over the age of eighteen who have to take a certain number of classes and also work at the studio answering phones or doing clerical chores. They sometimes tour and do live shows to get dancers used to being in front of an audience." When they've completed their work-study program, they're ready to meet agents and start to work. And work is what it's all about for Salgado, who suggests that if dancers are going to take classes, they should consider taking them from choreographers who may be in a position to hire them. "It's all about relationships," she offers.

Salgado is always developing relationships with casting directors, who've come to respect her business savvy. The musical *Rent* is a good example. When Salgado was at Bobby Ball, "the casting director blocked a full day for our clients and asked us to send in people every five minutes for eight hours. We booked five immediately on the first audition." Six months later they called the agency, asking to see a new batch of performers. "But I knew there were singer-dancers they'd met on the first audition who were perfect, so I made an executive decision and sent a handful of clients they had already seen. They were thrilled. They wanted to fly them to

New York immediately." She wasn't afraid to tell them the truth, that they had been passed over the first time around. "I love it!" she gloats. And if you're a performer who loves this business and wants to succeed, Salgado insists it's positive energy, talent, and the ability to maintain a good rapport with people that will be the deciding factors. "Give them the best you can, so when you walk out the door, you feel good about yourself. If they like you and don't use you now, there's always next time. If the rapport was there, you're in!"

Judy Savage

THE SAVAGE AGENCY
6212 Banner Avenue
Los Angeles, CA 90038
(323) 461-8316
FAX (323) 461-2417

From stage mother to theatrical agent, Judy Savage is one of the most recognized names in the Hollywood community. Managing all three of her children's showbiz careers certainly taught her the ropes and gave her the contacts she needed to start her own successful career. Did she have a clue when she was taking her talented son on auditions in Detroit that one day she'd have her own agency? She was too busy to give it a thought. At age seven, her oldest son was starring in *Oliver,* a precursor to his taking over the coveted child lead in the national touring company of *Mame.* "That's when I had to pack up my three children and go on the road for a year. That was thirty years ago. I finally sold my house in Detroit and moved west." By the time she arrived in Los Angeles, all three kids were working. Only when they got older did she decide she loved the business too much to quit. "It's funny. I was a pre-med major in college and never did anything with it." She laughs. "I never really could stand being around sick people." So while her youngest son, who was twelve at the time, was doing *The Tony Randall Show,* Judy Savage was starting her own agency.

Opting for a change of venue, each of Savage's three children went off to college and chose new careers. One is a composer, another the head of an editing firm, and the third a news reporter. And Savage has been helping other people's children and young adults build successful careers since 1978. "I struggled through writers' strikes, commercial strikes, and other tough times," she admits, "but the last ten years have been exceptionally good."

She has represented major child talent, and when someone questions the ethics of having children work at such a young age, she responds that it all depends on the family's attitude. "If children come from good families with good values," she says, "and don't think of this as their whole life but as a hobby they get paid for, they'll benefit. It comes down to parenting." When Savage interviews a potential client she always tries to find out if it's the child or the parent who wants this career. "If I ask a child what he or she likes to do most and the child says sing or dance or tell jokes, I know the kid really wants to do this. But when they say they love sports, you know they're not going to last. Sports will come first, and that's what they should do, otherwise it's the parent's dream."

When Savage began in the business, producers and directors would adamantly discourage kids from taking acting classes. As time passed, however, Savage watched many children fall by the wayside due to a lack of training needed to pull them through the transition to adult actor. "My kids were fortunate to work with such great actors as Bette Davis and David Niven," she says. "George C. Scott, who worked on a film with one of my kids, told me he would still takes classes any time he wasn't shooting a movie or doing a Broadway show." As soon as her clients are able to read, she gets them into a class. "I look for classes that involve relaxation, sensory work, improv, and scene study." Her favorite is Diane Hardin's Young Actor's Space in the San Fernando Valley area of Los Angeles. "When I first met Diane, she was teaching in a church basement. When I observed the students, I was in tears. Every scene was a one-act play. Every improv was wonderful. Of course I had to keep this training a secret from those casting directors who thought kids' acting classes only involved line readings. Ironically, good acting has absolutely nothing to do with line readings."

Savage is an advocate of ongoing training. Kellie Martin, who began as a child actor under Savage's tutelage, still takes classes and gets coached for auditions, even though she was a regular on *ER*. One of Savage's first clients, Chad Allen, who appeared on *Dr. Quinn Medicine Woman,* continues to study his craft. "The examples are myriad," she says. In fact, Savage often attends acting seminars touting her philosophy and finding talent along the way. "Rider Strong and his brother, Shiloh, were at a seminar Diane Hardin and I were doing in San Francisco. They were amazing. We encouraged them to come down to L.A. for pilot season, a trend I started. Now it has snowballed, and scores of agents have their clients come in just for the season." Savage believes it's easier for a newcomer to get a lead in a pilot than a small role in an existing episodic. "They're just willing to take more of a chance with pilots than with established shows."

The Savage Agency features eight full-time staff members, handling theatrical, commercial, voice-over, and everyday operations. Their clients booked sixteen pilots during a recent pilot season (an amazing figure), and of the 150 clients on their theatrical roster, half of them are working on a regular basis while the other half are in development and ready to go. "The kids that succeed most of the time," offers Savage, "are the ones who are so interesting you don't want them to leave. Jodie Sweetin, for example, could read at a college level when she came in for her first interview. At age five she was cast in an episode of *The Hogan Family.* She was so good she shot it in half a day. Immediately after the show aired, network executives called to set up a development deal."

Kids like Sweetin are an agent's dream. They're outgoing and talented. But what if your child is shy and yet has acting ability? Savage recommends commercial workshops and ten questions a day. "If you can just ask your child ten questions, it takes the attention off the child, develops focus, and teaches how to carry on a conversation. It's wonderful training to overcome shyness, which is the biggest thing that holds them back."

Savage believes it's never too late to get a child into the business. "Six is the ideal age," she says, "due to the child labor laws and the amount of time a youngster can work on the set." After age six, it gets tougher and tougher, due to the numbers trying to work their way in and the scarcity of roles. It often takes seven seasons before one of her clients will book a pilot. "One positive thing about starting later," she interjects, "is that the older they are when they start, the longer they seem to last. The little ones come and go. The older kids will stick with it five or six years and not give up until they start working." And while many young actors opt not to continue in the business as adults, like her own three children, Savage will help those clients who want to remain. "I have alliances with some of the larger adult agencies so that when they're ready to make the transition we can share these clients. In that way my clients can remain loyal to me and also satisfy their need to be moving 'upward.'"

Savage has a word of advice for parents: It's a big, big commitment on their part. "Parents may have to give up their jobs, because it's a law they be on the set with their kids. The crew often frowns upon stage moms, but there's no alternative. I try to get fixed sitter fees, but it's not mandatory, and some producers won't go for it. Parents are also responsible for ensuring that their children have a well-rounded life, and that all the attention doesn't go to their heads. They have to take care of finances. It's never easy, but it's vital that the parent keep the child's welfare in the forefront, because it's your child's attitude, not aptitude, that determines his or her altitude."

Mona Lee Schilling

CARLOS ALVARADO AGENCY
8455 Beverly Boulevard, #406
Los Angeles, CA 90048
(323) 655-7978
FAX (323) 655-2777

The Carlos Alvarado Agency was one of the first theatrical agencies in Los Angeles. Started in 1943, the agency was turned over nearly twenty years ago to Alvarado's niece, Mona Lee Schilling, who's currently in charge. "My uncle," she explains, "had no children. He had been in Hollywood since the silent movie era. He and his brother were friends of Rudolph Valentino. They all used to live in the same boarding house and used to steal milk from the milkman, because they were so poor." Schilling was approached by her uncle in 1981, after her husband had been killed in an accident. Her children were in college, and she finally had time to work outside the home. "I had been in the office for only ten days when my uncle became ill and never came back. I stayed on, even though I knew nothing about the business." Fortunately for Schilling, she had a photographic memory and learned quickly. "I'd look through my uncle's files of headshots and memorize what each actor did."

The agency was the first in Los Angeles to handle a large number of Latino actors, mostly principal players. Some of them, mostly character actors, have been with the agency since the '40s. "We handle about 100 actors, a few of them children. It's more difficult now than it was when I started," she admits. "Things started to change around 1990. New casting directors popped up. Old ones retired. The studio security got tighter. I couldn't walk on the lot anymore to say hi to people. I had to start doing more on the phone." Today it's all phone, fax, and computer, she sighs. She does submissions through Breakdown and Castnet and gets sides for her actors online. She hardly ever leaves the office, which is now located in a less-trafficked area of Los Angeles. "We used to be above Book Soup [a popular newsstand-bookstore] in West Hollywood. It was an interesting area. I remember this guy who kept coming in and asking for representation. I told him we couldn't really help him. One day he just started to cry. I finally had to call the police, who told me the guy had done the same thing at other agents' offices. By the time the police arrived, he had disappeared."

Schilling insists that actors who drop in or have an appointment be considerate to the person at the reception desk. She cannot abide rudeness. She recalls an elegant gentleman who paid a visit to her office unannounced and proceeded to pester the receptionist for an appointment until Schilling had to come out and yell at him to leave. "After I left, the actor grabbed his photo and resume from the receptionist and told her he had better things to do than wait around the office. That is obviously not an actor I'll ever want to see again." Schilling says an actor should understand the importance of being friendly, but not too friendly, especially at auditions. "Casting directors are very busy people," she insists. "If you try to spend too much time chit-chatting, it can be annoying. They may feel that if you're taking up so much of their time, you might do that on the set, too." A more professional attitude is to get there on time, know the sides, deliver the material, and leave.

Schilling tries her best to help Hispanic actors get work. She recommends good acting schools and tries to submit against type to casting directors. "Unless it's a big name, though, it's very hard for them to break in." She has been successful, however, getting her clients roles on *Angel,* a Hispanic takeoff on *Charlie's Angels,* and *The Brothers Garcia,* a new series about a family in Texas. "It's very gratifying when you have actors you believe in finally land a nice part and get going."

Schilling often has actors come in for cold readings. She also likes seeing demo tapes. "I don't want actors sending in tapes that I don't request, however. I'll just end up throwing them out." If an actor doesn't have enough credits to warrant a tape, Schilling is still open to discussion, but once she has signed someone, she insists they start putting one together as soon as possible. It provides her with yet another sales tool, and the more sales tools available, the more chance an agent has to get an actor recognized.

Some agents don't require a contract, but Schilling expects actors to work with her on an exclusive basis. "I work hard for my clients, so I do want loyalty on both sides," she insists. There are slow times for the agency, and she hopes actors understand it's not necessarily the agent or the actor, but that the industry is cyclic. Of course, if you're a teen or in your early twenties, you have a better chance of avoiding "down time."

Schilling has seen the industry go through several changes since she assumed control of her uncle's agency, but despite the ups and downs, she maintains a positive attitude, which she hopes to transmit to her clients. "If you love it, you just have to persevere. If you don't—well, there are other careers."

Sandie Schnarr

SANDIE SCHNARR TALENT
8500 Melrose Avenue, #212
West Hollywood, CA 90069
(310) 360-7680
FAX (310) 360-7681

Sandie Schnarr is a pioneer. She was the first to take the risk of starting her own agency to represent only voice-over actors. It started fourteen years ago when Schnarr was working at the revered Los Angeles commercial agency Sutton, Barth and Vennari (SBV), one of the most prestigious voice-over agencies on the West Coast. She was a receptionist with dreams of gaining admittance to the voice-over department. The good news was that Schnarr's dream came true: She became an agent at SBV. The bad news was that three years into the job, she became ill and had to take nearly a year off to regain her strength. During that time she decided that instead of returning as an employee, she would take the plunge and start her own business. "I actually had someone co-sign a loan, and I became office room-mates with an on-camera agency. We split the rent and the receptionist. It worked out great. The very first woman I signed was doing KABC promos within a week!"

It's an interesting story, exemplifying Schnarr's skills as an agent. When Kathye O'Brien was referred to her for representation, Schnarr says they hit it off imme-diately. "I really liked her, which is very important to me. Talent is great, but if I don't like the person I'm going to be working closely with, I'll pass." Schnarr happened to be talking to Rick Swanson, one of the producers of television promos at KABC, while O'Brien was in the office, and Schnarr mentioned her name. It seems O'Brien was married to an old school buddy of Swanson's, and he had met Kathye. It turned out that O'Brien was perfect for the job which lasted for years— not a bad start for either woman.

Voice-over agents work somewhat differently from colleagues who handle on-camera work. Many voice-over agents, including Schnarr, have their own recording booths and engineers who put their clients on tape and deliver the reel or cassette to the advertising agency producing the commercial. "A lot of us have the same contacts, but some of us have our own contacts we've developed over the years, including advertising agencies, casting directors, and writer-producers. What calls we get just depend on who likes us and who doesn't." The process begins when the ad agency sends Schnarr the commercial copy and lets her know what they're looking for: age range, attitude, voice quality, and so on. "Then we decide which of our actors fit the category, and we bring them in for an audition." It's similar to the process at the voice-casting studios, which often act as middlemen between the ad agency and voice-over agent. "It's a lot harder for an actor to get on tape at voice-casting studios. The voice-casting companies are hired because the advertising agency doesn't want to have to listen to 750 people, so they may bring in only 15 actors for an audition, and you may never have a shot."

If you do get selected by a voice caster, however, you have a better shot at getting the job. "That's because when I get copy, so do ten or so other voice-over agents who are all going to submit maybe twenty people." Do your math, and you get the point. A perfect example of the extent of the competition is a regional television spot for which Schnarr was asked to submit a couple of years ago. "It was for a local telephone company in northern California. They didn't know if they wanted a male or female, so that increased the numbers right away. I sent in at least thirty actors' voices. The job was coming from a casting office in San Francisco, so of course all the talent agents in San Francisco were also submitting. I happened to be visiting a talent agency in New York that week, and I discovered that New York was also in the competition. I couldn't believe it, and when I talked to the casting company in San Francisco, I asked her what was up. She said the call also went out to Chicago. All that for one regional TV spot! They had to have listened to at least 1,000 voices."

When Schnarr takes on a new client, which is admittedly an infrequent occurrence, it helps to have a good range. "I don't want to have a department of 300 or more voices, so my standards are very high. I know that no one can do it all, but it's nice if they can do commercials and animation, or announcing and promos." The business has changed, though, and some actors today are making six-figure incomes with just one voice. "It's more an actor's field today rather than an announcer's realm. Maybe they're looking for a gentleman in his fifties with a homespun storyteller quality. They won't hire a young guy who can do an older voice. They want an honest feel. If I get a script asking for somebody in their mid-twenties, that's who I'll bring in. It's not a sound anymore, it's an attitude. Someone who's forty-five isn't going to have the mindset of somebody twenty-three." What Schnarr is looking for is more of an emotional rather than a chronological range. "If I'm getting copy for a twenty-year-old nerd, I'll bring in my hip, young, sarcastic twenty-year-old guy who can also act nerdy. I'm not going to send a forty-year-old voice-over actor who can sound twenty. It just won't work today."

Another highly competitive field is animation. It's so competitive today mainly because it's dominated more and more by celebrities. "There is also a core of animation actors who get used over and over again, because they're so versatile and work in this specialized area all the time. We're always told they're looking for new people, that they don't want to hear the same old, same old. But look at the credits, and tell me they're seeking new voices!" Of course there is a need for voice-over talent in other areas besides commercials and animation. According to Schnarr, there is a lot of CD-ROM work today, as well as industrials. Unfortunately, much of that work is nonunion, and Schnarr will only work on SAG and AFTRA projects.

Audio tapes are a must for the voice-over actor, not only to get a good agent but to keep ahead of the competition. "Say an ad agency doesn't have the time to send us a script. They'll call and ask if I have any actors who might be right for the spot, and if my client has done a good tape mailing, I'll just ask the producer to listen to so-and-so, and they can book the spot just through a good tape." Schnarr has a list of 4,000 people to whom actors can submit. While she doesn't expect every actor to send out thousands of tapes, she does suggest they send out at least 300 to 400. "There are times I'll get a call from somebody who wants to book one of my people. When I ask how they heard of the person, they say through a tape or CD. It happens a lot." A well-edited two-minute tape displaying an honest, believable voice is best. "You don't necessarily want four thirty-second spots on it, but you don't want five-second clips either. Perhaps eight or nine spots, some slightly longer than others, so that the person listening can get a good idea of the actor's style."

Schnarr is optimistic about the future of voice-over. "It's always going to be there. There'll always be commercials. People always want to sell their products." The problem is that the group doing the work is more select every year. "I've been in this business a long time, and there's a small group of people who get the most work and earn the most money. But these working actors are very good. I think the one thing in voice-over that's probably true in any field is that if you don't book the job, there's someone better than you. It's that simple. There are better scientists, better car dealers, and better voice-over actors. That's life. It doesn't mean you're not good. There's just someone who may be better. In order to survive in this business," Schnarr emphasizes, "you have to accept that fact of life."

Ron Singer

FILM ARTISTS ASSOCIATES
13563 Ventura Boulevard, 2nd floor
Sherman Oaks, CA 91423
(818) 386-9669
FAX (818) 386-9363

Some people know from the outset exactly where they want to go in their pro-fessions; others rely on serendipity. Ron Singer is one of those who became an agent not through guidance and careful planning, but through happenstance. He was a personal manager in New York when he began his career. One of his favorite clients, legendary jazz singer Shirley Bassey, was performing in Los Angeles, and that's when Singer decided the West Coast was where he wanted to settle. When the disco era hit with a bang and lounge acts virtually disappeared, Singer turned to managing actors and soon after to agenting. "It seemed a more direct way to handle actors, dealing with the casting directors and setting up appointments. I like taking a managerial approach to my work. One of my clients is currently leaving the Ashland, Oregon, Shakespeare Festival after ten years to work on Cameron Crowe's upcoming film." Singer had successfully submitted the actor for several episodes of *ER*. "When he was down here for the second *ER*, I had him audition for Crowe. He has fourteen weeks on the film."

While Film Artists Associates is a full-service agency above and below the line, Singer handles only theatrical. Other departments include commercial, lit-erary, and young people. The boutique agency caters to not more than two dozen clients at a time. "And the clients I select have to be over eighteen and gorgeous," he quips. But seriously folks, Singer relies on his own formula: P-A-T. "It stands for personality, attitude, and training. Those are the three ingredients I look for in an actor. I look carefully at the resume. I've been shot down by casting direc-tors too many times by handling clients with insufficient credits. If you're over thirty and have few credits, no matter what the excuse, you're simply not going to be seen. It's just as much a problem for newcomers as it is for stars who've dropped out for a few years and try to make a comeback." He cites the example of Russ Tamblyn, a well-known theater and film star of the '60s who made a brief return on the cult television favorite *Twin Peaks*. "He wanted me to manage him, and I tried. But I couldn't even get him arrested. Going off to New Mexico for ten years hurt him."

Singer enjoys sharing his years of experience with up-and-coming actors. He often lectures at his favorite acting workshop, taught by Bobbi Chance. "The first thing I tell them is what I'm looking for from actors: chocolate donuts!" He wants actors to know he's a friend. He's not the antagonist that many perceive agents to be. Aside from donuts, Singer tells actors he needs tape. "Without a good video, I can't judge the actor's ability. I always ask for tape. Sometimes I do it to get rid of an actor, too," he admits slyly. "If there's no chemistry with an actor, and the person won't leave of his or her own accord, I'll just say to get some tape and come back. They usually don't bother." He knows all the tricks, the ones he uses as well as the ones casting directors use. "When I call casting directors to follow up on submissions and they tell me to fax them a photo of one of my clients, it's a brush-off. If they're interested, they'll call me or ask me to send my client in for the audition." Singer also mentions casting directors who "dump" calls. "They know if they call you back at lunch or after seven, they can just leave a message and avoid a conversation. They do that all the time. So what do I do? I'm usually here during lunch and after seven."

Cover letters to agents are critical, according to Singer. "Never do mass mailings using 'Dear Sir or Madam' or 'To whom it may concern.'" He has a file filled with cover letters, exemplifying the best and the worst. Even when a photo and resume don't grab him, if the cover letter is clever, he may call the actor in. "But before you look for an agent, you have to do your homework by going through agent guides or the Academy Players Directory to find out which actors are with which agents. Find out if there's a pattern, if certain agents handle a certain type of actor." When you're interviewing with an agent, Singer suggests asking such questions as how large a client list the agent has, how he or she sees you as a type, how many actors on the roster are similar to you, how the agent handles communication, and how accessible the agent is. "An agent who tells you he or she doesn't believe in conflicts probably has a number of similar actors in the same category. The question is how many, and how will you be marketed?"

Singer cannot abide clients who aren't honest with him. He wants every actor to call him immediately after an audition to let him know how it went. "But I want the truth. So many times an actor will tell me how great it went, and there's no callback. Then I hear from the casting director that the actor didn't do very well. I'd rather be lowballed. Tell me you don't think you got the job, and surprise me. I love that!"

Singer is well aware that this business is filled with subjectivity. No matter how well an actor does on an audition, it often comes down to a certain look or attitude being sought. He remembers a classic example of subjectivity that happened fifteen years ago when he was a manager. "I got locked out of an Equity waiver theater with a young actor. We started to talk. I liked him and said I'd try to help him find an agent. I did. I took him over to a major agency where he proceeded to mumble with a can of beer in hand. The agent got up, said thank you to me, and walked out of the room. The next day I sent him to Craig Wyckoff, another agent I knew. I got a call the next day asking why the hell I sent this kid. 'This kid has no idea what he's doing.' I had to tell the actor I couldn't help him, although I regretted it." The kid turned out to be Sean Penn, and whenever Ron Singer runs into Craig Wyckoff, Wyckoff asks him if he has any more Sean Penns. "We laugh. That's showbiz."

Susan Smith

SUSAN SMITH & ASSOCIATES
121 North San Vicente Boulevard
Beverly Hills, CA 90211
(213) 852-4777
FAX (213) 658-7170

When you enter Susan Smith's office, you feel as if she has invited you into her charming living room. The lighting is dim, the furniture is comfy. You're surrounded by antiques, and there's a fireplace across from her desk, all indications of a friendly atmosphere, not an intimidating one. However, one might be intimidated by Smith's wealth of experience as an agent. She has been in the business for nearly thirty years. "I was producing and casting commercials in New York, but then I was fired," she admits. "No one wanted to hire me as an agent, because I'd never done that. So I borrowed $5,000 from the man I was going to marry and opened a tiny office on 42nd Street without a single client!" But it didn't take her long to accumulate a formidable list of actors that garnered lots of attention. "The kind of people to whom I gravitated were unusual, to say the least. I have an off-beat eye; well, actually, two offbeat eyes," she jokes. Some of her "discoveries" include Glenn Close, who she spotted in a play in which Close just happened to be understudying that evening. Mary Beth Hurt was performing in a workshop at the Public Theatre, and Lane Smith was doing Off-Off-Off-Broadway. "In those days in New York, the only criteria was one's talent."

Smith is still devoted to talent. Even though she's now located on the West Coast, she refuses to become a typical "Hollywood" agent. "I realized the business was heading west, so I moved here in March 1974," she explains. And she operates in her inimitable style. "I don't answer to other people. I work for myself, along with five other agents." The agents work as a team for the ninety or so clients they represent. The work is divided up by studios, casting directors, and networks. Each agent has a specific area on which to focus, and each takes into account the entire client list when submitting recommendations. They're not looking to find new clients at this time, since it's Smith's belief that in order to do the job right, you have to focus on a limited number of actors.

Actors needn't submit headshots and resumes to Susan Smith & Associates. Clients are primarily referrals from lawyers, casting agents, and directors. "You have to have a body of work that I can see to make me want to represent you," Smith explains. "Unless you're sixteen, and we sit and talk, and I think you're adorable, and I don't have a sixteen-year-old on our client list, then maybe I'll consider you." That's not to say the agency represents children. She's just interested in finding good talent, and if that person happens to be a teen, so be it. "A casting director looking for somebody who is totally gorgeous is not going to find that here. There are dozens of other agents to call. But when you get actors from here, they may not get the job, but they'll always be excellent. Everyone out there knows that. That's our reputation."

Smith is not afraid to make phone calls. "I'll call almost anybody, whoever is the right person to help facilitate something I really believe in." She personally reads the scripts that may be submitted without a specific actor in mind; or sometimes the script is offered to a client such as Kathy Bates or David Paymer. "I read everything, so I know what I'm talking about when I'm dealing with both the actor and the producer or casting director." She also has no qualms about getting on the phone to get feedback on her actors. "I submitted an actor for the lead in a film about the life of Janis Joplin. I know she's an extraordinary actress, but I also knew she wouldn't get it. I didn't need to make a phone call to the casting director, but I did. They told me why she wasn't being considered, which was precisely what I already knew, but I was able to relay that to my client. Some actors need feedback. Others don't."

All actors, however, must act in a professional manner, especially nowadays, according to Smith. "Today actors must look their best, show up on time, and be prepared. The competition is stiffer than ever. Their pictures and composite tapes must be of a higher standard than ever before."

It's obvious that Smith is an iconoclast. Where most agencies represent more men than women (since there are more roles for men), she has an equal number of males and females on her roster. "It's probably not intelligent from a business point of view, but there are so many talented actresses, and I get along well with women. I know it has always been tough for them and will always be tough."

It's not the size of the role that is of primary importance to this agent; it's the quality. Smith recalls an instance when she received a script for Brian Dennehy in which they assumed he'd play a major role. "There was a two-day role that I preferred, and I told Brian. I faxed him the scene and told him which role I would take. He called me right back and said, 'I don't know why you even asked me. You're right, as always.' That's what it's like working with someone for twenty-one years!"

The most important job for an actor, says Smith, is studying your craft. "That's one of the things I love about Brian. He goes back at least every other year to do a play for almost no money, just to be in touch with what makes him an actor." Kathy Bates is studying screenwriting so that she can better understand the actor from the writer's point of view. That impresses Smith. And Smith apparently impresses her clients. Most have been with her many years. She's accessible and knows where each one is every day. "Actors need that," she stresses. "They need the reinforcement that you're really there for them. And I am, and always will be."

Peggy Taylor

PEGGY TAYLOR TALENT
1825 Market Center, #320
Dallas, TX 75207
(214) 651-7884
FAX (214) 651-7329

Peggy Taylor started her career as "makeup artist to the stars." Those stars included Bob Hope, Billy Graham, and Greer Garson. Today Taylor is the foremost theatrical agent in Dallas—a strange transition, perhaps, but it worked for Taylor. "I was always on the set," she explains. "I knew the business, and there were no talent agencies in Texas." That was in the '60s. "Finding talent was really a matter of the director getting a station announcer or someone he or she knew to do a voice-over, or putting somebody's mom or dad on camera." One day, while she was applying makeup at a television studio, the general manager asked if she knew someone who could be a hand model for a commercial they were about to shoot. She provided a name, and the general manager handed her a stack of photos and asked her henceforth to keep tabs on talent. The timing was right, since Dallas was becoming a popular mecca for nonunion film production. "The major markets were losing business to us, because we were willing to work cheap," she admits. "The little book I had started at the TV studio just started to grow." It didn't take long before the unions came into Dallas, and talent decided to organize to compete on a national scale. Taylor was influential in helping SAG and AFTRA acquire signatories and members.

What perturbed Taylor most about the business in Dallas was the proliferation of agency scams, which still exists, but thanks to her and a handful of other agents, it's much less insidious. "It's awful for actors when agencies open their doors only to sell photos and offer classes for a lot of money. They're rip-offs. They have no intention of getting actors jobs." She and other agents in the state were finally able to push through the Texas Talent Agency Act, requiring agents to be bonded and licensed. This act closed twenty-four rip-off agencies the day it went into effect, and Taylor is proud to have been one of those responsible.

This tenacious quality has kept Taylor in the forefront of Dallas entertainment for over thirty years. She admits she's a workaholic, up at 3:00 A.M. most mornings to do all the paperwork that seems to accumulate in her office. She gets so inundated, she occasionally loses track of her actors. Bill Thurman, an actor who has been with Taylor for many years, recalls the time he was shooting the film *Alamo Bay* with Ed Harris on the Texas coast. "She had to call my wife," he laughs. "She wanted to know where I was. She couldn't remember she had sent me on the picture!" Like Thurman, other actors have been with Taylor from the beginning of their careers. James Mosley has been with her since the '60s; he was cast in the original *Bonnie and Clyde,* and more than twenty-five years later, Taylor is still finding him work. Other clients have moved on, like Robert Urich, Melissa Martin, and Morgan Fairchild. "Morgan was known back then as Patsy Calmes. They needed a pretty lady to sit in a car for a commercial. I sent her out on it. That was her first professional job."

Whether an actor has credits isn't as important to Taylor as what those credits are. "We need versatile talent who can do more than sing and dance or be a cowboy. If actors don't have many credits, that doesn't mean I won't represent them if they have potential. I may even approach someone in a restaurant because of a special look." She's particularly interested in finding more minority clients with training and ability, as well as more talent of every variety who understand the art of marketing. "If actors don't do it for themselves, it probably won't get done," she insists. "I don't just represent a single actor. I have a fiduciary obligation to everyone I represent, and I can't single out one person over another. Actors should be their own salespeople. It's okay to take tapes and headshots and leave them with clients, to invite people to showcases, to send thank-you notes after each audition—things that are socially proper in any business." She tells actors to learn the art of networking. "That doesn't mean you should go to a cocktail party and hit everyone in the room with the fact you're an actor looking for work. Be polite, not pushy." She also recommends community theater, seminars with casting people, and acting classes.

Taylor tries not to overlook any talent when going through the daily breakdowns. She has her headshots up on the wall arranged in ten-year age spans from the youngest to the oldest. When the breakdown asks for a man over fifty, she'll go to the appropriate age bracket on her wall and decide whom to submit. "I had an actor once ask me what type I thought he was. I told him that I try not to think of people as types, because it would close my mind to other opportunities. But that's not to say actors should ignore the personal image they project. There comes a time when they need to choose a direction, even if they're versatile. If you have a flare for comedy, that's what should be developed. When actors get too far from what they naturally are, it becomes difficult to do a good job. I don't want them to hurt their careers by wishful thinking, believing that they're leads when they're really character actors."

The most rewarding part of her job is the relationships Taylor establishes with her clients. She gets business from Houston, San Antonio, and Austin, as well as from outside the state. "We've furnished talent for companies in Oklahoma, Louisiana, and California when they're here to work." She loves the camaraderie of the business. "We're like family. Everyone makes an effort to work together. I'm proud of everything they do. We're the most kissy-kissy, huggy-huggy industry in the world. Most people are open and affectionate. It's really fun and I love it."

Steve Tellez

CREATIVE ARTISTS AGENCY, INC.
9830 Wilshire Boulevard
Beverly Hills, CA 90212
(310) 288-4545
FAX (310) 288-4800

Nearly every newcomer to a large agency has to start in the mailroom. And yes, the cream does rise to the top. It happened to Steve Tellez, who began his climb twelve years ago in the mailroom at the William Morris Agency. "I didn't really know what I was getting into. All I knew was that it sounded exciting." The real excitement was when Tellez left the mailroom in a record six months' time, moving up to dispatch and ultimately to "the desk." But the agent to whom he was assigned wasn't in an area of interest to Tellez, and he became impatient. His decision was to become a big fish in a small pond, and off he went to a smaller agency to get his feet wet. "They told me, 'Go be an agent. I don't want to see you back in the office until four o'clock.' So I did. I'd go and make the rounds of the studios, pull out my clients' pictures, see what was being cast, and hopefully make the deal."

After a number of moves from small to midsize agencies, Tellez wound up at one of the most prestigious agencies, Creative Artists Agency (CAA), where he has been for the last five years. "It's not for everyone," Tellez admits. "We're into building careers. It's more long-term here, and we work as a collaborative team." When an agent from CAA spots an actor in a small festival movie, he or she will bring up the name at the next meeting, and all the agents will discuss it. "What we want to do is find someone who can break out and become a star. Is this a person who'll listen and take our guidance? I think you have to be open to every possibility. If you hire an agent, you should listen to your agent." Tellez offers advice to a number of clients interested in making the move from television to film or vice versa. "Take Nashville superstars like Reba McEntire or Garth Brooks, for instance, who are grossing close to the top with record sales and tours. We try to find a script that will take their personality and translate it onto the screen, to find a balance between what the artist's needs are and what the network wants and hopefully make everyone happy."

This is packaging, something agencies like CAA are very good at, and why major stars want to come aboard to take the next step in their careers. "I think packaging is one of the most misunderstood words in the business," says Tellez. "It's so different with TV and film. With film it's more about having a piece of material with the right director or actor and shopping it around. With television there are package fees, license fees, and the like. It's taking a writer's idea and focusing on the network, figuring out what the need is and starting to build around it." In the case of Reba McEntire, for instance, Tellez was able to find a film for her, *Forever Love,* and place the costar (Tim Matheson) and director (Michael Switzer) in the package and sell it to the network, satisfying a number of clients all at once. "Packaging is really taking a project from its inception and seeing it through the entire process from network meetings to reading every draft of the script to intelligent conversations with your client and the network, balancing everything, and even on the set, making sure it's all running smoothly. It's not just getting the project sold. It's keeping it on the air."

Creative Artists Agency primarily represents name talent, and the main focus in the acting category is on youth, since that's today's market. CAA does not have a commercial department. They do, however, represent writers, directors, and producers as well as actors. "We're a team. We work very closely in terms of how we make our decisions. We'll identify those we feel may be the next wave. Someone may have attended a comedy festival in Montreal or Aspen, or a manager will call and say we have to be at the Improv at eight o'clock to see someone. If you like what you see, you discuss it at the next meeting, show some tape, and make a decision." It's a highly selective process. While CAA may represent upward of one hundred clients, each agent may only handle ten to fifteen on a daily basis. "We all work together for each client," Tellez explains. "We simply figure out in any given situation who the best agent would be to make the call. There's a strategy involved in every move we make. We use our entire force to help a specific situation or get an answer to a specific question."

Tellez expects his clients to keep in touch with him on a regular basis. "I think it's important for them to speak to me. It's a gauge. It's all hills and valleys in this business, and I think all actors go through this, and they need to communicate with their agents to see what's going on. Let's face it, they're depending on you. It's important to have that communication." He claims to have that rapport with clients like Mary Stuart Masterson, Jack Lemmon, Sissy Spacek, and Gary Sinese, and he's excited about their careers and how he can perhaps expand their horizons. "If there's one trend in the business today," says Tellez, "it's the movement of an actor from one medium to another or from actor to director. A lot of it is based on choices. You don't have the old labels of being only a television star, just as agents are no longer TV agents or feature agents. The smart ones do everything. They have to be aware across the board of what's going on in all areas including books, music, theater, everything. It's the big picture we're looking at."

In Tellez's opinion, actors are their own worst enemies. "You end up getting in trouble by overanalyzing situations and eventually backing off from taking a risk. If you're not willing to jump in and do something that just might be different, even when your agent suggests you give it a shot, it's harmful. Sometimes you have to go with your instinct. Your first instinct is always the correct one, but it's when you get caught up sitting on the fence too long, all of a sudden the opportunity dissipates."

Trusting your agent is imperative. The relationship must have give and take. "The toughest part of my job," he admits, "is adjusting to each client I'm speaking with. They all have different fuses, different demeanors, and different ways of communicating. It's an art." It's also an art being able to choose the right clients. "It's not that it's so mysterious, but it's really about talent at the end of the day that shines through. I've seen people come from little independent movies or stage plays in London or on Santa Monica Boulevard. As an agent you have to be responsive to what's going on in the industry. It means going out there and looking." And once you find each other, you listen to each other. What does the actor want from the agency? What does the agency expect from the actor? "You should be able to get as much information and as much advice as you can. You should use an agency for what they have, and that's information. That's the most valuable tool you can have in this business."

Bonnie Ventis and Jody Alexander

KAZARIAN, SPENCER & ASSOC., INC.
11365 Ventura Boulevard, #100
Studio City, CA 91604
(818) 755-7570
FAX (818) 755-7553

If you talk about children's representation with any casting director in Los Angeles, one of the first agencies mentioned is Kazarian, Spencer & Assoc. (KSA) and its celebrated kid's department, under the dual direction of Bonnie and Jody. (Their last names are often superfluous in the industry). The two have been working with children at KSA for ten years, and they don't plan on changing their focus. "Children maintain their priorities," says Alexander, "unlike adults. A birthday trip to Disneyland is often more important than an audition. That keeps us honest and makes us understand there's a world out there, instead of getting so wrapped up in what we do on a daily basis. We're constantly being reminded that kids must be kids, which is important."

KSA's children's department represents about two hundred young actors of all ethnicities; but despite the numbers, Ventis and Alexander don't feel they have too many actors of the same type competing with one another. "It's so competitive out there already," says Alexander, "we don't want it that way in here. We consider ours to be a boutique department with large agency clout." They find their youngsters primarily through referrals. "Managers and casting directors speak highly of us," Ventis proclaims. "We also go to showcases and keep our eyes open at all times. Even though we may take off our agent hat when we leave the office, we never stop looking for talent." She recalls taking a lunch break on a trendy street in West Hollywood and spotting a cute ten-year-old boy, whom she approached. "Unfortunately I found out he had just signed with another agent!" That's Hollywood.

Don't think because the turnover among child actors is high that Ventis and Alexander are desperate. They're not. "We want the best little actors we can find," Ventis stresses. "We won't take someone on just because of their looks. They have to have at least the potential caliber of the best of our bunch." And it's not always easy to find. "Seems the whole world is looking for eight- to ten-year-old boys, because girls apparently want to act and dance more than little boys, who prefer sports." Another "hot" category is the sixteen-year-old "drop-dead gorgeous" guy or girl. Ventis and Alexander will bring in young actors who fit a category for which they have an opening and have them do a cold reading. "We give them a script to work on for a few minutes," Alexander explains. "Ten minutes later, they do the scene for us. Sometimes they get it right on the money, and those are the kids we take."

All actors have to audition at KSA, even if they're discovered at a showcase and have impressed the agents with their performance. "We just never know how long they've rehearsed that scene," says Ventis. "In order for us to know how they'll perform at auditions, we have to bring them in and have them do a cold reading." They hope to see that sparkle and energy they spotted at the showcase. If the actors have that, as well as a desire to pursue the business, Ventis and Alexander will sign them. If their acting is a little weak or they need to hone some skills, Ventis and Alexander will simply refer them to one of their favorite coaches, such as Dawn Jeffrey Nelson, Sean Nelson, Mia Hack, or Stacey Meltzer. "Some children, however," adds Ventis, "should never be coached. They're perfect the way they are, so why mess with their innate ability?" For other kids, it depends on the difficulty of the script. Sometimes they'll send clients to a coach just to get their comfort level up, so they'll know what's expected of them when they go on an audition. Actors who are too young to read are given improvisations to perform. The agents will also make sure children are able to memorize simple material for the times they'll be reading for a commercial that has dialogue.

Another important aspect of representing children is the child's own desire to be in the business. "We will not sign someone if we feel the child doesn't want to do this, and it's only the parent's dream," Ventis emphasizes. This brings up the subject of stage parents. "We had an instance when one of our five-year-olds was on a callback not too long ago. The waiting room was near a vending machine, so the mom said she'd get him candy. While she was away, another mother went up to the little boy and berated him, telling him he had no business being there, and that her own child was going to book the job. Our client was so upset, he didn't even want to go in and read with the casting director. The casting director was surprised at his attitude, since he had done so well on his first audition. After talking with the child, the mom found out what happened and explained it to us. Unfortunately, it was too late."

If a child is just starting out in the business, Ventis and Alexander recommend snapshots, since 8x10s are expensive. Children can use photos taken by a family member until the parent is ready to invest in professional headshots. "We also need our clients to communicate with us at all times," Alexander insists and recommends a beeper, always equipped with fresh batteries. "Our kids have to be ready to audition pretty much at the spur of the moment and must understand they're making a commitment to us." If an audition has been postponed, they'll immediately let the parent know, and in turn, they expect parents to notify them when they're going to be out of town or otherwise unavailable. "It's embarrassing," says Alexander, "if we tell a casting director we're submitting a client, only to find out that the child is going to be on a field trip that day."

Ventis is not happy with one aspect of the business that she feels has made it very difficult financially for families. It has to do with a change in the Coogan Law that originally mandated that a producer had to put 15 percent of the gross the child earns into a trust account that cannot be touched until the child turns eighteen. "Now the courts are demanding a higher percentage be set aside to the point where it's now a third of the salary. So today, a family can go into the hole. They can be out the $258 dollars earned. The agent gets 10 percent. The manager takes 15. A third is for the trust. They're in a 50-percent tax bracket. If something isn't done about this, only millionaires will be able to afford to be actors!" Ventis and Alexander have attended meetings at the Screen Actors Guild to discuss this problem, and they say SAG is trying to find a solution.

Despite the difficulties, thousands of families are still eager to have their children participate in film and television, and when asked, Ventis and Alexander recommend the traditional approach to avoid getting ripped off by unscrupulous charlatans, of which there are many. The first thing to do is get a list of franchised agents from SAG or AFTRA, take clasp snapshots of your child, write a letter to the agents expressing your desire to find an agent for your child, and include date of birth, height, weight, and skills. "But be careful with those snapshots," Ventis suggests. "One parent felt her child should be dressed up for her photos, so where did she stage her photo shoot? We noticed the child was centered right in front of a coffin—at a funeral! We passed."

Kristene Wallis

THE WALLIS AGENCY
1126 Hollywood Way, #203A
Burbank, CA 91505
(818) 953-4848
FAX (818) 845-2437

Kristene Wallis certainly followed an unusual method of finding a career in show business. She had a friend who was a facialist, and one of the friend's clients was the wife of the owner of a successful talent agency in Los Angeles. Apparently Charles Stern wasn't happy with his assistant and was seeking someone to fill her shoes. "It sounded like fun, so I applied," Wallis explains. "I wound up being with Charles for seven years."

The Charles Stern Agency exclusively handled major celebrities for voice-overs and commercials, as well as a handful for theatrical. At the time, Stern was spending an average of two hours a day in the office and traveling quite a bit. Since the staff consisted of just him and Wallis, within a few months it became clear that someone other than Stern had to do the recording of in-house auditions. The problem was that Stern apparently had no intention of teaching Wallis that end of the business. Then fate took a hand. Wallis recalls the first time she had to do a recording, which turned out to be a major feather in her cap. "We had an important client who needed to get an audition on tape immediately. Charles was out of town, and I knew if I didn't do it the client would lose the job. We worked together to try to figure out how to use the equipment. When Charles got back in town, he was floored, but I had a new career." The clients were the ones who actually taught her how to use the audio equipment. "In order to understand how to direct, I decided to take a voice-over class myself from Wally Burr, a well-known producer-director, who years later became my husband. Hey, who says showbiz isn't romantic?"

Wallis eventually grew tired of only handling celebrities. She wanted to explore new talent but didn't have the freedom to do that; so she moved on, establishing a voice-over department at the acclaimed Gold Marshak Liedtke (as it is currently known), which until her arrival had only represented actors on camera. "I worked there a year, until they couldn't afford me any more," she explains. On her own for the last six years, she's still the voice-over connection for Gold Marshak, but now she handles not only voice-over actors, but the on-camera side of the business as well. "My heart has always been in theatrical," she admits, but adds that it wasn't easy for her to break into that area. "It appeared to be next to impossible, until one day someone told me to simply stop using envelopes and cover letters with my submissions. It worked. As soon as I started putting those little stick-on notes on my piles of photos, it happened." Casting directors were starting to take notice of Wallis's on-camera clients. "My messenger service was happy, because we were saving trees."

Due to of Wallis's expertise in audio recording, most auditions for voice-overs are done in her office. She credits her former boss, Charles Stern, for being the first to establish an in-house audio studio. "I really prefer the on-camera end of the business, though," she confesses. "When I'm running a voice-over audition, I'm in the booth for hours and can't be on the phone drumming up business. And if I'm lucky, I get one booking after all that work. With theatrical, all I have to do is send out photos, make follow-up calls, and wait for something to happen." She can also submit more people in any given category in theatrical, whereas in voice-overs she's limited in the number of actors she can submit on tape, due to time restrictions. "My true love is theatrical and always has been, but I will always have a voice-over division, simply because I'm one of the few agencies in town that does, and I've been very successful with it."

Wallis isn't as interested in what actors look like as she is in their talent. "I only handle fine actors," she proclaims. "The vast majority are character actors, as opposed to the young glamour types." She also limits her submissions to those she knows are right for the part. "I'll even talk a casting director out of seeing a client if I don't think the role is appropriate. If they tell me what they're looking for, and I know my client can do the job, I'll tell them. They love it. I'm honest and won't make a fool out of an actor or waste a casting director's time." When she sends an actor out on an audition, she knows what that actor can do. "Before I represent an actor, I usually have the person do two scenes or monologues for me. If I've seen the individual in the theater then I already know what he or she can do, but I always ask to see a tape, if it's available." When Wallis has actors do a scene for her, she'll usually give them adjustments and ask to see it again to discover how they take direction. "I've rejected people based on what they've done in my office. If I see some potential, I advise them to take classes to bring their skills up to speed and invite them to come back later and try again."

Wallis also finds voice-over actors in theater. "I remember going to see *Bouncers*. It was very intense, with all the men speaking with a cockney accent. I interviewed one of the actors after the show and found out he was Canadian, not British. He was so good with dialects, I represented him for years." In fact, Wallis is known for representing voice-over actors from all over the world. "It started when I got a call from a voice-over director seeking an Icelandic actor. I had to track one down at a bar where people from Iceland get together. I talked to the bartender and found out that not only was he Icelandic, he was a famous DJ back home." He booked the job, a feature film with Steven Segal.

While bars may not be the best place for actors to meet agents and casting directors, cold reading or networking workshops are, according to Wallis. "It's not that I prefer finding actors at a showcase, but for actors, it's a great way to meet industry pros. It works. I just booked two actors on *The Practice* because I saw them at a workshop." Among the workshops she recommends are Reel Pros and In the Act, because the caliber of actors who attend is very high. "It's important to go to professional-level workshops. You certainly don't want to be the best actor in a room with lousy ones. Casting directors will wonder what you're doing there." Another piece of advice: "If you believe in your talent, don't give up. I've had several clients who did nothing for three or four years, and then they took off. Of course, once they started making six figures," she laughs, "they left me." She also cautions actors not to pin all their hopes on the agent. "It's your business," she warns. "Your agent isn't going to do it all for you, but if for some reason you're not happy with your agent, you have to be honest. Don't be afraid to speak up for fear of being dropped. You have to take control of your life if you're going to succeed."

Jadin Wong

442 West 57th Street, #5J
New York, NY 10019
(212) 757-4794
FAX (212) 262-0118

A tour of Jadin Wong's Manhattan office reveals a photo of her at twenty-three with Humphrey Bogart and Lauren Bacall, as well as personal dedications from Bob Hope, Orson Welles, and Frank Sinatra. There's also a framed copy of Wong on the cover of *Life* magazine from 1940. You see, Wong was a performer at the Forbidden City, the first Chinese night club in San Francisco. Then, during the '50s and '60s, she appeared in such major Broadway hits as *The King and I*, *The World of Suzie Wong*, and *Flower Drum Song*. There weren't too many prominent Chinese-American women in the entertainment industry in those days. Her film career goes back a long way, too, with roles in the classic *Charlie Chan* and *Mr. Moto* movies. Even today, Wong, now an octogenarian, still appears occasionally in commercials and television shows.

Nowadays, however, she's known more as an agent-manager than a performer. She's perhaps one of the most powerful theatrical agent-managers around, representing hundreds of Asian-American artists for nearly a quarter of a century. Wong deals only with ethnic actors. Her career change came about almost accidentally when the Tony Rivers Agency, which represented her, was closed due to fire. She agreed to take the phone calls during the transition, and she really enjoyed it. "I was only supposed to answer the phone," she recalls. "But people kept calling and asking for actors. One lady said she needed Indians, so I went to all the agencies and brought her 150 pictures." Since it wasn't customary to use Native-Americans, few had headshots, so Wong had to be creative. "I cut out pictures from *National Geographic* magazines and pasted them on the resume." They got booked.

When Tony Rivers returned to take control of the agency, it wasn't long before he told Wong he was quitting. " 'You ruined my life,' he said. I asked him why. He told me he was now making money for the first time and didn't even have time to go to the bathroom." She continued to work part-time, helping him with ethnic casting. It finally just became too time-consuming to pursue on a part-time basis, and Wong became an agent. Today she represents between 500 and 600 ethnic actors—including Chinese, Koreans, Tibetans, and Malaysians—and handles actors from infants to fellow octogenarians. "I get about twenty or thirty pictures a week. I go through them and decide whom to call in. I only sign a few people. The rest work on a freelance basis." She also finds actors in more unusual ways. "Once I discovered a heavily bearded man reading [a newspaper] in the subway. He was a teacher. I went over and talked to him, and he booked a few commercials."

Working with Asian actors is a challenge for Wong. "There aren't the number of roles available to them," she admits. "There's little chance of landing the romantic lead or juicy role. Those parts are just not being written for Asians." But when they are, Wong is there with her roster. Whenever there's a theatrical production, movie, or television show requiring Asian actors, she usually gets the first call. "I just wish the roles were more substantial," she bemoans. "I have an actor who works all the time, but even with the flurry of callbacks and residual checks, the breadth of roles is narrow. A few years ago, for example, he appeared as a dancer inside a Chinese dragon for a fast-food commercial. He played a catering chef on a sitcom, a cook on another TV show, and a hairdresser in a commercial." The actor's favorite, though least lucrative, role was that of an Asian broadcast reporter in a repertory theater production.

Another factor Wong must take into consideration when dealing with the Asian community is the innate shyness and sensitivity. "You have to learn how to talk to them in a different way than you would with other ethnic groups. I'm always telling my clients to remember to smile at commercial auditions. They're looking for outgoing people. Asians, on the whole, are not usually outgoing people." She'll even encourage a client to attend a commercial workshop if she feels the actor would benefit from it. "For the most part, they're looking for real people. You don't need a lot of training for commercials. But if I think a person has a future in this business, I'll recommend acting classes."

Wong often has to educate those who utilize her services. "The Chinese language has twelve dialects. Most Caucasians don't know that. I have to keep telling casting directors you can't mix dialects. It's just not real." She laughs as she recalls a recent call from a casting director. "She asked me if I had an 'impy' Chinese actor. I couldn't think of any. That is, until I went to a function at the Chinese Historical Society. I ran into the famed architect I. M. Pei. Suddenly I realized they weren't looking for an 'impy' Chinese man; they were looking for someone who looked like I. M. Pei! If I hadn't gone to that party, I would never have known."

Wong's life in theater, and as a proponent of Asian-American performing artists, has played such a crucial role in the history of entertainment that both Lincoln Center's public library and the Museum of Chinese for the Americas have begun establishing collections of her life's work. A documentary, *Forbidden City*, focused on her nontraditional career. It isn't common to see someone at Wong's stage in life putting in the hours she does. She could rest on her laurels, but of course Jadin Wong is not the average woman. "I certainly don't do it for the money. I keep doing this at my age because I like people. We're a family here." She continues to dance and exercise every day to keep in shape—to be ready for the next casting call. As for her clients, they have to love the business as much as she. "When people come to me and say they want to be rich and famous, I tell them to get into computers. If they say they want to be an actor because they love it, that's special. They have to have the passion for it, like I do."

Craig Wyckoff

EPSTEIN, WYCKOFF &
ASSOCIATES, INC.
280 South Beverly Drive, #400
Beverly Hills, CA 90212
(310) 278-7222
FAX (310) 278-4640

There was a time when Craig Wyckoff would sign just about anyone who could act. You could be fifty years old without a union card, but if you had the ability to deliver lines, you'd have representation. That was then, as they say, and this is now. Wyckoff has moved from his original Hollywood Boulevard digs of the '70s to his plush Beverly Hills office of the new millennium. But even though his location may have changed and his clients may have become more select, Wyckoff is still the dedicated agent he was when he started twenty years ago. Partners have come and gone, but Wyckoff has been able to keep his agency flourishing through thick and thin.

At the moment, things are thick for this agent, who began his career as an actor himself. "We've finally lost our boutique status," says Wyckoff of his agency's growth in the last couple of years. "We have three agents here on the West Coast who represent more than ninety clients, and during pilot season we have an influx of actors from our East Coast office for whom we're obligated to work, so we're no longer a small operation." Indeed, actors with tape get bicoastal representation. "Even if you're based here in Los Angeles, New York people are seeing your work on tape." One client, Robert Miano, got a starring role in *Donnie Brasco* with Al Pacino after submitting a tape to the East Coast office. "He sent his tape back there, and they hired him."

When Wyckoff began his operation he had twenty-five clients. His philosophy was that it didn't matter what type you were if you could act. Today, he's somewhat more businesslike in his approach. He now takes into account factors such as marketability and credits, because the overhead of running offices on both coasts means he can't afford to have an actor sitting around waiting for a break. "We write up appointments for each actor that go into his file," he explains. "At the end of the year we look at each file to see how many auditions the person has had." Figuring that it costs a few thousand dollars per year per actor just for basic representation, Wyckoff concludes, "If I'm losing money, we have to cut the cord." And what exactly is marketable to Wyckoff? "We look for people who are very established character actors or young, beautiful men and women," he answers. "The better looking you are, the easier it is. If you're a character actor, we have to scrutinize your acting a lot more, unfortunately."

That's not to say that beauty alone will cut it for Wyckoff and his staff. "We had a guy come in recently who was the best-looking person any of us had ever seen," he recalls. "He was in his early twenties, one of the most marketable age ranges, a gorgeous creature, but there was nothing interesting about him. If he almost put me to sleep, can you imagine what he'd do in a casting office?" When Wyckoff passes on an actor, he'll tell him or her that there's a "conflict," which simply means there's another client in the same type and age range. "That's a polite phrase that means we're not interested," he confesses. "The reality is, there's no such thing as a conflict. I send up two clients for the same role all the time, and they compete with each other. The only time I think there's a real conflict is if one of my actors feels there is."

When Wyckoff believes in a client, he'll get on the phone at 9:00 A.M. and start selling. "All agenting is a sales job," he admits. "I sell people. I have to know my product. I have to know my buyers, like any other rep selling to a company. I know most casting directors personally. If they try to tell me the actor isn't appropriate, I try to convince them that he or she is, and remind them of recent credits. Selling the actors usually works. We have a good batting average." When an actor's average, however, begins to fall, Epstein, Wyckoff & Assoc. will often have to let that client go. Also, when personalities clash or if an actor is simply unprofessional, there'll be a parting of the ways. "I don't want to work with someone I don't like," says Wyckoff. "If a client has been missing appointments or not picking up material, I won't stand for that. Or I'll work hard to get an actor in to read, and right before the audition he calls to tell me he's been out all night partying; can I change it? I don't get it. When I was an actor, I was a professional, and I can't understand that attitude."

As far as managers are concerned, Wyckoff has a working relationship with more than sixty of them. "Some are a real help and are important to an actor's career," he admits, "but others I have to laugh about. All they say is, they've read about a role in Breakdown, and wouldn't this be right for my client? Believe me, I see the same Breakdowns, and I'm their agent. Thanks for taking up my time to tell me what I already know." The good ones, however, will call Wyckoff and say they saw a particular project in Breakdown, and they know the producer. They'll have called the producer and will inform Wyckoff that the casting director will be calling him shortly with an audition. "That's an effective manager. Or one who will advise the actor which offer to accept careerwise versus moneywise, or arrange a luncheon with a producer or director."

It's time-consuming always to be holding an actor's hand, but Wyckoff is more than willing to talk to his clients if they drop in to say hello. "A lot of agencies don't like that," he says. "We tend to work in a more managerial style with our clients. We give advice, discuss careers. One actor came with us at the beginning of his career, and we stepped him through episodic TV to movies of the week to a series and guided him along the way on what he should and shouldn't do. He was afraid to turn down any work, and I had to advise him that he was at a point in his career that doing just episodic was not a smart idea. He didn't see it, until one day he was doing an episodic and wasn't available for a screen test for a major feature. He finally understood what we'd been telling him, and he changed his attitude about his career."

Indeed, Wyckoff's own background as an actor is a double-edged sword for his clients. "Having been there, done that, is both my downfall and saving grace," he explains. "The saving grace part is that I understand actors, and we're actor-friendly in this office, but I'm also a little tougher on actors. I know a lot of the nonsense they present." He laughs. "One of my clients is the biggest pain in all of our butts, and he knows it, but he's also my favorite, because he's a brilliant actor, and I respect his talent." He shrugs. "He's working on himself as a person."

ADDITIONAL RESOURCES

Agents on the Internet

With the Internet such an integral part of our lives nowadays, many actors assume that having their headshots and resumes online is the way to go and that "snail mail" is a relic of the twentieth century. Unfortunately, finding an agent is not yet a process that can be fully achieved online. It's true that you can have your photo and resume accessible online through the Academy Players Directory and CastNet, but you're still going to have to write an old-fashioned letter to the agent or agents of your choice, since most of them aren't fully equipped with web pages and e-mail for the general public.

If you're fortunate enough to have been invited by an agent to submit online, you can simply forward your material via e-mail, but most actors have access only to agents' business addresses, which are easy to come by, for a price, at any theatrical bookstore. Some lists even provide address labels, so you don't have to bother typing out the information yourself. Since you're going to have to send a letter to the agent anyway, you might as well include that headshot and resume. Informing them that your picture is online may only thwart your purpose. That extra step may be one too many for a busy agent.

Through my research for *Agents on Actors,* I have been unable to find a website that provides more than a listing of agents across the country. A few agencies have their own sites, but those that have them do not solicit submissions from actors. Of course, this may change during the next few years, or perhaps sooner. The Internet is quickly becoming the primary means of communication in many areas, including show business. On the whole, casting directors were reluctant for a long time to relinquish personal control of submissions to online services. Now it's pretty much the standard. Will agents follow suit? Only time will tell.

As of early 2000, when this book went to press, the sites that may be helpful to actors were as follows:

1. **aftra.com-resources-agencylist.html** This site lists agencies in various markets of the United States that are franchised through AFTRA (American Federation of Television and Radio Artists). Information is organized alphabetically for each state and includes the basics: name, address, and phone number.
2. **sag.org/agentlist/agentlistindix.html** Another list of union-franchised agents across the country, this too is categorized by state.
3. **actorsite.com** This website has a short Q&A section on the difficulties of finding an agent. It also reiterates some of the things contained in this book.
4. **theatrgroup.com/showbiz/agent** A good source for actors on many basics, including agents franchised by SAG/AFTRA and SAG/AFTRA offices nationwide.

That's about it. If there's a particular agent in whom you're interested, you might try to locate a webpage through your search engine. While you probably won't be able to contact that agent directly online, you'll at least be able to find out a little more about the agency. If you're good at surfing the web, you may be able to come up with other websites in the future. I know I'll be looking, too.